Ecclesiastes Speaks to Us Today

Lawrence W. Bottoms

John Knox Press
ATLANTA

Bottoms, Lawrence.
  Ecclesiastes speaks to us today.

  1. Bible. O. T. Ecclesiastes—Criticism, interpretation, etc. I. Title.
BS1475.2.B67   223'.8'07   78-71053
ISBN 0-8042-0104-8

This book is dedicated to our children Lawrence, Jean Leticia, Janice and their families in the hope that our grandchildren will experience the new humanity in a world where human reason begins to understand what the Sage is saying to our age.

Preface

The Book of Ecclesiastes contains the reflections of a philosopher about life. Life is dynamic and moves toward its goal. Anything which is against life is against God and anyone who is against God the Creator is against life. Anyone or anything which is against life fails and cannot reach the goal of life, which is to live.

This philosopher, or Sage as he is called, is trying to achieve the goal of life by the use of reason alone. He examines and questions many of the accepted beliefs and traditions of his culture.

He seems to ignore that man is created to live on three levels as an integrated whole in order to achieve the true goal of life. He has a body; he has a mind; and he is a spirit. Man becomes a living soul through the breath of God.

The reader will need to understand that when the word "man" is used in this book, that the word refers to the whole human race, male and female, created in the image of God in a relationship of reciprocity.

The word "man" is used in faithfulness to the creation account and is faithful to revelation and redemption. Our understanding is that we are created in the image of God. Unity is important and in their deeds the whole people and God move toward the future together.

The Sage, by reason, keeps discovering that life is not

achieving its goal. All is empty—vanity—a breath. Reason leads the Sage to think life is not worth living.

In Chapter 12, verses 9 and 10, the author is described as a sage, a teacher and a skillful writer. Only in chapters one and two does he assume the literary role of Solomon.

No attempt is being made in this book to deal with Ecclesiastes verse by verse on a critical basis. This kind of verse by verse study has been done well in the *Layman's Bible Commentary*, the *Expositor's Bible*, and in other commentaries.

In this book the author is calling attention to the basic questions that underlie all of life. The book introduces themes whose elaboration is still in process and whose development still brings joy, sorrow, and understanding to our lives.

The book will be better understood if read with child-like simplicity, as if reading or listening to the tale of the master storyteller who understands that fundamental human existence has not changed. That which helps life to achieve its goal is still just what it has always been. In the beginning, God created man and breathed into him the breath of life . . . man became a living soul . . . that is still the way it is if life is to achieve its goal.

It is the hope of the author that the book will speak to you so that your life is fulfilled.

And now I wish to express my profound thanks to Dr. Richard Ray and the staff of the John Knox Press for helping me express this message in readable form and to Mrs. Margaret Montgomery for her typing.

None of the ideas expressed in the book are original with me; however, I take full responsibility for the message as I understand it.

—Lawrence Bottoms

Contents

Chapter 1	The Problem of the Book Is Stated	11
Chapter 2	The Search for the Best Good in the Realm of Wisdom	27
Chapter 3	The Search in the Realm of Pleasure	40
Chapter 4	The Search for the Best Good in the Affairs of Business	46
Chapter 5	A Better Way of Worship Is Open to People	62
Chapter 6	The Search in the Realm of Wealth	76
Chapter 7	The Sage Rechecks His Experiments	88
Chapter 8	The Quest Achieved	96
Chapter 9	The Problem Is Solved Conclusively	102

Chapter 1
The Problem
of the Book Is Stated
ECCLESIASTES 1:1–11

The Sage, speaking in this book, is trying to find human
fulfillment within the limits of human reason. The search
for the Chief Good is the theme of the Book of Ecclesiastes.
In the first chapter, the third verse, the writer wants to
know, "What does man gain from all of his toil under the
sun?"

The seeker of the best good by human reason does not
deal with the question, "Why should one be Christian?" for
he lived before this question was viable. His concern is with
the question, "How can one be truly human within the limits of reason?"

Since the Sage was a member of a group which tried to
find the direction to life in wisdom, he investigated this
question of being human and tried to answer it as concretely
and practically as possible within the horizons of his times.
Thus we should keep in mind the experiences and conditions of the century and of society in which he lived.*

In that period people thought that the earth was flat, that

---

*For information concerning this period of biblical history, see A. B. Rhodes, *The
Layman's Bible Commentary*, Vol. 10 (Richmond: John Knox Press, 1964).

the sun was above the earth, and that heaven was above the earth. They reached for human sagacity that would enable them to cope with the natural problems they experienced. In the course of doing this they dealt with the basic question, "How can one experience fulfillment and be fully human without God?"

Is there something more to the question of life than simply being human? The people of wisdom did not want to deal with that issue in the experiment which the Sage had set before himself. We wonder why. Had suffering led them to take God out of the equation? Or had they feared that the question of God might cramp their style of living? Did this lead them to rule him out in the very beginning of the search? Perhaps all of this was involved. Interestingly, we see that it was not necessary to deal with a moral code for living. They would have to deal only with the legal codes for living. In a very real way, they took only an empirical or scientific method in their search. This was life "under the sun."

People who lived life in this fashion eventually began to feel unfulfilled. They were aware of the fact that they had forgotten past generations and they were sure that future generations would forget them. This knowledge made them unhappy.

The Sage observed that the sun ran its race across the heavens and returned the next day as a fresh young man to run its race again, but the unfilled person who had experienced no self-actualization would die and be forgotten. This was an unhappy state of affairs.

The Sage observed the wind. The variable and inconsistent wind which blows where it wills, blowing through the same quarters and the very circuits which have been its course in ancient generations, returns and blows in its same course in the present generation.

The streams which ebb and flow, which come and go, running out through the streams and rivers into the ocean, return to the clouds and come down as rain again. The sassy little brook can say to man, "You cannot do this."

Man shifts from change to change. Compared to the calm uniformity of nature, his life is a mere fantasy. All is empty, for man has no fair exchange for all of his labors under the sun, no surplus on the balance sheet of his self-actualization. The Sage concluded that people will die and be forgotten. That was the mood of the age.

The sentiment of these eleven verses in the first chapter is that all of the natural elements and forces, even the most variable and inconsistent, renew their strength and return upon their course. But frail man—look at him! For frail man there is no return—no self-actualization, no fulfillment. Permanence and uniformity are the character marks of the natural elements, while transitoriness and instability are the character marks of man.

The society in which the writer lived was described, analyzed, and examined, but life with God was not examined and defined. The fact of God was constantly in the background and was a reference point of the inquiry of the sage, but life with God was never seriously examined by the Sage at this point in his experiment.

The Sage, no doubt, thought of his age as the modern age. It was an age of science. Science said that the earth was flat. It was the age of technology of an elementary kind. Men followed orderly methods in getting things done. It was an age of culture. They built public works, parks and the like. They had places of culture and entertainment. Still, in spite of all of this, it was difficult to deal with the question of humanization.

The religion of Israel and the history of Israel, as far as the Sage was concerned, had had their day. The God of Israel was dead as far as this experiment in humanization was concerned. Religion was bankrupt. The wisdom of the age was the thing of the hour.

This is somewhat like our day at a time when people believe in the pantheism of process, planning, and management. This kind of process is limited to the wisdom of man for fulfillment, social action, and justice. Even though our wisdom is helpful in all of these areas, we must remember that it is God who calls for social action and justice. He calls us to what we might describe as truth in action. God is truth. This means that wherever God is left out, truth is left out and where truth is left out, full humanization is impossible.

The people of the author's day wanted above all the "Best Good," but they were not interested in the truth of wisdom above the sun. They did not want to be superman, but at the same time they did not want to be sub-man. They wanted to be completely *man* in a world as human as possible—made human by human reason. The Sage was a pragmatic, practical person who believed in and wanted a "secular" world. He perhaps would say, in this experiment, we are dealing with a "worldly" world.

The issue is human pragmatism versus divine pragmatism. In the early part of the book, however, the Sage rules out divine pragmatism. He will not deal with that in the book until much later, after human pragmatism has failed often enough to make him look above the sun.

The vital issues of human pragmatism are self, power, and survival. The sage is aware of life around these vital issues and consciously or unconsciously, he is forced to deal with the basic needs of being human in order to be a self with power in order to survive.

You and I are aware of the basic needs required in order to be human. The Sage also must have had some knowledge of the broad base needs that seem to be the universal motivators of human behavior.

The basic needs which motivate human behavior, according to some recent psychologists, can be ranked in the following way:

First: Physical needs or biological needs
Second: Safety or security needs
Third: Social or love needs
Fourth: Ego or esteem needs
Fifth: Self-actualization or self-fulfillment needs

It is important that we realize that psychologists isolate and list these needs for purposes of study. Actually, people are not divided in this manner, for people are an integrated whole. They are not dominated for any length of time by any one single need. Most often people are motivated by a complex web or combination of needs which manifest themselves in a variety of ways. It will, however, help us to understand ourselves and the Sage better if we look at our basic needs and understand something of their hierarchy.

In the more developed nations it is unlikely that many people ever really encounter a deep-seated physical need for any length of time. Physical needs include the biological requirement for food, drink, air to breathe, shelter from heat or cold, and the need for sexual satisfaction. It is important to remember that these are the most primitive needs of people. People will kill to get water. They will even resort to cannibalism to avoid starving. A drowning person may become absolutely mad in a scramble for air to breathe.

The physical needs are in some sense of the word the strongest. They are also satisfied more quickly. These are the needs that must be satisfied if life is to be sustained. Only in unusual instances can other needs occupy a person's mind and dominate his or her actions when these basic physical needs remain unsatisfied.

Safety needs are also important, but only in emergencies such as a riot is a person likely to encounter a basic fear for life and safety. Such situations do not come too often. We usually encounter people's safety needs in more subtle and disguised forms. Safety needs are included in a person's insistence on fair play. If people feel that there is no justice in their day to day encounters, their safety is threatened because there are no rules on which they can depend. Needs for security are shown in a desire for job tenure, for job protection, and in a desire for insurance protection.

The only real security, however, lies within the heart and soul of the individual person. It is eternal. This kind of security deals with a person's ideas, attitudes, values, and commitments. Ultimately each person is responsible for his or her own sense of security, understanding that security is in God alone.

One of the greatest motivators in the behavior of any person is the quest for social acceptance—for belonging, for association, for friendship and love. These are the needs that prompt people to want bigger homes, bigger cars, clothes, and money. These things are modern-day symbols of social acceptance.

The need that people have for social acceptance is usually an outward manifestation of a deeper need. The real need of people is self-acceptance. Again this need points to value systems which should come from God who accepts us because he loves us.

Ego needs are our next concern. The ego needs are essentially needs for self-respect. They are the desires of the individual to feel that he or she is a worthwhile person, making a contribution to life which is significant and satisfying. Our ego needs are not satisfied if the acclaim we receive is not deserved. On the other hand, we do not need to have public applause in order to satisfy this need. So long as we know ourselves that we have achieved this need for the glory of God, the need is gratified.

The final need is the self-fulfillment need. People's self-fulfillment need is the search for continuous growth and self-development—for progressive realization. God has planted eternity in the hearts of his creatures. They will not be satisfied until they "find their rest in God."

The self-fulfillment need comes to the forefront of attention only after all other needs are moderately satisfied. This need cannot find optimal expression while a person is hungry, fearful for safety, or feeling rejected.

As a consequence, the struggle that most people experience is that satisfying these other basic drives generally dilutes and directs their energies away from self-fulfillment. Most people, therefore, experience limited opportunity for this last, but all-important, need.

People fail to seek first the rule of God in their lives. They have been too busy. God has been ruled out. Therefore, the Sage keeps coming up empty in the area of self-fulfillment needs.

People kept working in a "worldly" world for the lower needs in an effort to be human while still wanting the highest basic need for self-actualization. They wanted this highest basic need but they ignored the source of this highest basic need.

In a "secular" world, people endeavor to deal with humanization by developing political and legal solutions which keep turning out to be nothing but band-aids for the ills of society. They develop good legal codes, but they have no moral codes for they do not work for moral solutions. The Sage kept experiencing emptiness in his experiment as we keep experiencing emptiness in our social experiments.

They had no God and no moral solution even though God was constantly present in the background calling for a moral solution. Because of his love, God was continuing to give the Sage an opportunity to choose life rather than death. The Sage kept limiting his experiment to the path of emptiness. By his limited experiment he kept choosing death.

Because of man's choice, his character and information which he was willing to use, it seemed that the natural elements would vanish and disappear and return. The sun seemed to sink; the winds lull; the streams run dry; but they all come back again. But for man there is no coming back. Once gone, he is gone forever.

The mood of the day concluded that there is no need of talking about human fulfillment—such talk is vain—the band-aids do not heal the weary, restless, secular, worldly society. Man cannot alter it. All through this "secular," "worldly" society what has been still is and will continue to be. There is no new thing under the sun.

The Sage and the people of his day must have tried to make laws to improve society. They believed in law and order and tried to motivate people by fear. However, fear motivation is always negative. Furthermore, smart people could always figure ways to get around the law.

The Sage and his people would also use *incentive motivation*. Where fear motivation uses punishment to improve society, incentive motivation uses rewards to improve society. This kind of motivation has its limits also. People become slaves to external forces and cannot experience the attitude motivation which operated outside the areas of authority structures and laws. The Sage could know nothing of this kind of freedom which produces self-actualization because this kind of freedom comes from God who is truth in action. God and truth cannot be limited to political solutions in a worldly world.

God is a creative being and he calls us to live in a creative relationship with him in a configuration of others, order, and reciprocity. This order of living calls for forgiveness, service, and the renunciation of power which controls. They are the vital issues of life. This is the kind of world in which people are free for self-fulfillment and creative living.

In a world in which the vital issues are self, controlling power, and survival, emptiness becomes the repeated cry—all is vanity, says the Sage.

The Sage concludes that there is nothing new under the sun. We know better, for they did not have Ford Thunderbirds in that day. No man, in their experience, had gone to the moon. People were failing because they did not know the Creator and neither did they understand how they were created.

No new experiences can come into our lives when we are governed by a basic fear of the unknown. Fear causes a natural resistance. Fear and faith cannot exist in the same heart at the same time. Faith, love, and confidence root out fear by the process of replacement. There was no faith in the God of love, so since the people of the Sage's day had had no inward experience of anything new, they tried nothing new externally because they were afraid that they might be incapable of performing effectively. As bad as the present situation was, fear and the habit of negative thinking kept them from entering into any new set of circumstances. Any new situation or circumstances which affected them individually and disturbed them personally were avoided. There was nothing new under the sun because people were creatures of negative habit caused by fear. They could not be people of faith because they had no God.

The approach to social living and the experiment of the Sage were governed by people who knew little or nothing of the full nature of God. The significance of the One who is the creator, God the Father; who is also the generator, the Son; and at the same time who is the activator, God the Holy Spirit, was unknown to them. They had no knowledge of God in these functions acting as an integrated whole.

The God they had left out of their lives was the one God

in whose image they were created. They too were to live as
an integrated whole. All of their basic needs were to be acted
out in an integrated whole. Perhaps it might help if we considered the *hierarchy of needs* as an example. We can put it
like this: their physical needs, safety needs, social needs, ego
needs, and self-actualization needs were to be lived out in a
relational, integrated manner. Yet they failed in integrating
these areas. As a result, they were completely unable to meet
their own highest need. People were unfilled because they
remained caught at the level of their lowest needs. They had
no faith in God who was ready to help them move progres-
sively toward social action and justice, which are truth in
action. Like Pontius Pilate, who is a characteristic figure of
one who is caught by his negative fear, they expressed the
attitude which carelessly says, "What is truth?"

When people can live in creative cooperation with truth,
even commonplace things become new. This was the experience of the woman at the well, because Christ had gen-
erated a new source of life in her. She broke with old,
negative habits when Christ, the generator, the Son of God,
was sent by the Father, the originator, for the purpose of
helping people experience life as an integrated whole. God's
purpose is the well-being of all people. People who live under the sun miss that purpose in their experience with life.
Life becomes empty. The Sage wanted "well-being" but he
kept missing it because he rejected the purpose of God in
his experiment and test of life.

The commonplace task of daily social living through a
social organization can become new when we bring to that
task a new, creative personality, a personality which is new
from living with the creative, living, personal God. The commonplace task becomes new because we become new, growing personalities. Such people have a new understanding of
being responsible to God for their own personal and social
goals.

God calls us to live and grow to these social goals in the framework of social arrangement of forgiveness and service. We are called to renounce the power which dominates people's lives. Emptiness of life was experienced because people did not accept the plan of God for living.

You will do well to realize that the Sage rejected the account of God in Genesis. In Genesis we hear, "In the beginning, God . . . " In Genesis the writer is setting forth the relation of the world and particularly of man to God. The most important thing for any individual to remember is his or her personal and social responsibility to God. People are created in the image of God. In their relationship to one another—man and maid—they are called to function as an integrated whole in social organization of agape.

Genesis is not trying to prove the existence of God. The writer is simply telling the story of God's relation to the world and people.

The writer of the Book of Ecclesiastes rejects the story of Genesis and tells his own story. He describes what the world and life are like when people reject the Genesis story.

Return to the Genesis story again. Man is a person standing at all times in a personal relationship to God. It is this relationship which constitutes him man.

Whether people know it or not—whether they like it or not—people are distinctively persons at all because they, in the innermost core of their being, are in a right relationship with God. People are persons because they are in touch with and receive a word from the eternal God.

The essential truth to understand is that all things in existence are the creation of God and that God works in an orderly, progressive and purposeful manner. All things have been called into being out of nothing by a ruling, intelligent, and originating, creative Being. God is active and his works are orderly, progressive, and purposeful. The sun rises because God commands it to do so. The sun is obedient and responsive to God. By the sovereign will of God, natural laws are the descriptions of the dependable consistency of God.

People sometimes miss that truth. The Sage of Ecclesiastes missed it. Not only is this the experience of people way back in history when this book was written, it is also our experience in our time. In our time, we do not think of the world as being flat, but in our own way, we try to live without God. So we do well to understand the mood of the Sage. His heart was heavy with the memory of many sins and many failures, the result of living without the God who preserves and sends judgments.

The wise philosopher had ruled out of his experiment and life the God who created, the God who brought the children of Israel out of Egypt, the God who keeps covenant "to a thousand generations."

Not only did the wise counselor rule God out of the experiment by ignoring his certainties of action, he also ignored his certainties of relationships.

The Sage, as a child and counselor of his age, addressed his contemporaries. Not only does he speak to his age he is speaking to people of every age.

The Sage is a man of ripe wisdom and mature experience and he takes us into his confience. He opens up the secret volume of his heart and invites us to read it with him. He shares with us what he has been, what he has thought, and what he has done. He wants us to know what he has felt and suffered and then he asked us to hear the judgment which he has deliberately formed after he reviews the whole experiment which he had conducted "under the sun." We are told that he uses the poet's privilege and presents himself to us under a mask, wrapped in the mantle of Solomon.

He presents himself as a man who is weary with many futile efforts and endeavors. With what remaining strength he has left, he tells us of his despair. It was because his heart was heavy with the memory of many sins and many failures and because the lofty Christian hope was beyond his reach that this man of wisdom grew mournful and bitter with his life and its lack of fulfillment.

The wise counselor does not understand sufficiently well the vital issues of his problem. He applied himself to search for understanding about everything in the universe. He discovers that the lot which God has dealt to him is not a happy one. It is all foolishness and chasing after the wind.

From our time and advantage in history, we can understand that even though the Sage was wise, he was foolish. He used the sophisticated wisdom and realities of his day but yet he did not use all the wisdom available to him when he limited his thinking to things under the sun.

The writer perhaps thought that in addition to the earth's being flat that it was also the center of the universe. Copernicus humiliated the humanists of his day by showing that the earth is not the center of the universe. Men who have walked on the moon now join others in telling us that the earth is a little speck in the universe. The Sage needed God for faith far more than he was able to realize at the time the Book of Ecclesiastes was written. We can understand that his conclusions had to be tentative. The Sage was not sure either for he was motivated by fear. His fears made him think he was correct in saying what is wrong cannot be made right. Fear and faith cannot exist in the same heart at the same time, so having little faith the Sage concluded that all is futile. In his fear-torn mind, he had the opinion that nothing is worthwhile. He did not seem to understand that this was only an opinion born out of frustration.

It is no doubt true that the course of the sun is pre-set. It is also true that animals cannot select their own goals and that their life is determined by built-in goal-images which we call instincts, but through information which we have today, we know that this is not true of man. People are goal seeking individuals—that is, they were created to be goal-seeking beings with thoughts, emotions, values, and attitudes. People will not live well until they have personal goals and social goals.

Perhaps the man of wisdom did not have this information, although he should have known from the Genesis story that people are called to individual responsibility to God. God created a world of abundance. He created man and woman with talents and abilities and he gave them the power of choice. They were free to choose the tree of life or the tree of good and evil. They were free to choose to consume freedom, to try to possess it, or be creative with God and produce responsible freedom. However, under the influence of evil and the urging of their lowest needs, they chose to be consumers of freedom. They failed to produce responsible freedom through the agape, or unselfish love, and personal leadership that would have existed in the configuration of others, order, and reciprocity.

We are always standing in responsible relationship with God. We are responsible for exercising a degree of genuine personal choice regarding the ways in which we are to live in response to God's call. Thus we must always face a creative tension in faith. On the one hand, there is the component of loyal obedience to God's will. Yet on the other, there is the freedom to choose our own personal goals under the purpose and providence of God.

We were made so that our goals would only be our own if they were personal and internal. Life is not genuinely fulfilled if others completely set the goals for us. Thus, to say it another way, we must be born again. We must come to personal maturity. We must begin to discover the breadth and depth of life when it is lived as a new gift from God.

This internal experience of personal maturity develops

a positive attitude towards life. We see it as open to new creative possibilities. This experience helps us to overcome the burden of doubt and to reject the negative, cynical perspectives about life that are inevitably crippling under the influence of evil.

This experience involves a basic change in our attitude towards God and in the expression of our own personalities. It is not to be oversimplified, for it involves both a developing rich fellowship with God and a different exercise of will and choice in human relations. For the symbolic language of the Genesis creation, it involves a walking with God in the cool of the evening. It necessarily includes the related step of learning to integrate the fulfillment of our personal needs. We develop, over an extended period of time, the will to balance these fulfillments while seeking to find the will of God for our lives.

The sage could have known about tangible goals and intangible goals from reading the story of Genesis, although he might not have called them by those names. We might, using our imaginations, think of it like this: We can delineate the possibilities of tangible goals through the use of our ordinary senses and our reason. On the other hand, intangible goals—thought of in this context as those appropriate to spirit–can be identified through the capacity of what we can well call our souls. In our experience with God, worked out through the breadth of life, our minds and hearts receive a new dimension. This is the dimension of new faith, love, and perception. With renewed perception, we look hopefully and joyfully to the positive features of human destiny.

The man of wisdom asked the question, "What does man gain from all of his efforts?" He answers his own question by saying, "Generations come and go but it makes no difference. The sun rises and sets and hurries around to rise again. The wind blows south and north and returns to run its course again. The rivers run to the sea but the sea is never full. The waters return to their source and come to flow into the sea again. Everything is utter weariness and empty. History merely repeats itself and in future generations no one will remember what was done in this generation of people who lost sight of man's destiny and God's purpose."

The Sage's heart was heavy with the memory of many sins and failures because the lofty Christian hopes were beyond his reach. He grew mournful and bitter.

This, then, is the mood in which the author begins his search for the chief good. He is driven to the quest because of the need of finding that in which he could find security and fulfillment. He wanted the good appropriate to the nature of man with all of his basic needs. In this mood the Sage begins to search while ignoring God.

Chapter 2
The Search for the Best Good
in the Realm of Wisdom
ECCLESIASTES 1:12–18

The Sage could not see the relationship between God who is in heaven and man who is on earth. What does religion have to do with wisdom? Perhaps in our times the question would be, "What does religion have to do with higher education?" Or "What does biblical faith have to do with secular humanism?"

We come up against this question in many different ages in many different ways. The human mind cannot get away from it. We are reminded over and over again that we must try to understand what it means to be faithful to God in time and place.

The Sage was dealing with his time and circumstances. The issue was the relationship between God and man. This relation is the theme of biblical faith. The Sage ignored this biblical faith.

Biblical faith insists that God created the world and that he gave people responsibility for its care and upkeep. We are responsible for the maintenance of both the physical environment and the world of human institutions—political, economic, social, and educational. The stewardship of the world is entrusted to people. People have a special responsibility to use wisdom and to understand that human learning at its best enhances human life. It helps to form the true life as God meant human life to be lived.

Another biblical insight is that we are saved by God's action and not by our own good works and intellectual theories. Our human ingenuity cannot bring our ultimate fulfillment. That is a gift to us from God by grace through faith. In this faith we use our wisdom and our work in behalf of the world according to God's purpose.

The good life—the common good of the nation—is discovered by trying to find the will of all of the people. The worship of God in the church is the people's way of discovering the will of God.

The elected officials of the nation represent a constituency. The elected officers of the church, however, are more. They are representatives of the Godly lifestyle. The national official is elected on the performance of political skills. The church officer, however, is elected on evidence of Godly living.

In the political life, the government proceeds from the will of the people to the ruler. In church courts and governing bodies of the church, however, we seek the will of God and attempt to follow his direction. In good government, the majority will recognize the rights of the minority. In the church the majority is also called upon to effect unity through reconciliation. The church is the light for the world.

This style of life came by grace through wisdom given from above the sun. It happens when the church makes the will of God known to the people and the nation discovers the will of God's people. This is the biblical pattern of faith.

The Sage proceeded to live a style of life which concluded that biblical faith had no place in the halls of wisdom. Being a wise person, the Sage turns first to wisdom. He gives himself to inquire into all the actions and toils of men. He works long, hard and earnestly at this task and acquires a "greater wisdom than all who were before him." This wisdom is not a scientific knowledge of facts or of social and political conditions and theories. Neither is it the wisdom which results from philosophical speculations.

The wisdom which the Sage acquired is born of wide and varied experience. He does not make an abstract study. He lives with people. He acquaints himself, through a living experience, with the facts of human life. He knows the circumstances, thoughts, feelings, hopes and goals of all sorts and conditions of people. He is determined to know what all people are doing "under the sun." He talks with servants, porters, merchants, tradesmen, artisans, businessmen. He looks with his own eyes and learns for himself what their lives are like, how they see their human condition, and what means they use to solve their problems. The Sage looks at the order of the universe and his depression grows worse, so he turns from the study of natural forces to the study of mankind. He finds this also a heavy and disappointing task. After a dispassionate study, when he has "seen much wisdom and knowledge," he concludes that man has no fair reward "for all his labor at which he labors under the sun."

None of this wisdom can set straight that which is crooked in human affairs. When people will not allow God to break through into their lives, that which is crooked remains crooked and that which is lacking remains lacking.

The feeling of emptiness brought on by his thinking of the steadfast course of nature only grows more painful as he remembers and reflects on the disorder which afflicts humanity. From our vantage point we can think about Christ who came to his own world and was received by everything except his own people. There is order in the universe but disorder in the affairs of men. People have gained a great deal of human wisdom. We still have to confess with the Sage that "even this is a vexation of spirit" for "in much wisdom is much sadness" and "to multiply knowledge is to multiply sorrow."

The times in which this book was written were times of cruel oppressions and wrongs. Life was insecure. The Hebrews as well as the conquering race which ruled were slaves to pride, greed, and violence. The fair rewards of honest toil were withheld. The noble were degraded and the foolish were exalted to high places through power politics. The righteous were trodden down by the feet of the wicked. There was no hope for a better life. These conditions only complicated and made worse the problem of living and brought on deeper brooding and despair. The thoughtful student of people and human affairs became sadder as he became wiser. "In much wisdom is much sadness."

Did not Christ, though full of grace and truth, share this feeling as he saw the publican growing rich by extortion? Would he have felt like this when he saw hypocrites taking the seat of Moses and in cruelty imposing laws upon people which they themselves did not keep? In instance after instance the scribes hid the key of knowledge, while the blind multitude followed their unseeing leaders into the ditch. Without a relationship to God, we have "eyes to see but we do not see." We have "ears to hear, but we do not hear." The truth remains that the "fear of the Lord is the beginning of wisdom."

Are our times any different from the times of the Sage? Look on our world today. Can we say that the majority of people are even wise? Can we say that they are pure? Is it not always the swift who win the race, and the strong who carry off the honors of the battle? Are there no fools lifted to high places to show with how little wisdom the nation is governed? What about the matter of honesty in the market place? What about frauds in our exchanges? Do the best people always gain the places of highest honor? What about the people of our times who have to suffer the oppression of delay because Christian people say, "It takes time." Have we ruled God out of our worship by living under the sun and accepting the culture because we believe in the oppression of delay? "Things cannot happen overnight" we say. That may be true from the viewpoint of human wisdom, but what about divine wisdom? What about the power of the resurrection?

From the viewpoint of the Christian, we do not begin our quest for wisdom apart from God, and we do not begin our quest for knowledge of God apart from faith. If we really want wisdom, we must begin with faith in the word of Christ, the word of God which has been spoken, and is being spoken, and will continue to be spoken.

If we are going to avoid living "under the sun" and rejecting God, we will find it necessary to take the Scriptures and the ancient confessions of the church seriously, for these Scriptures and ancient confessions are the highest expression of the church's faith. The individual Christian must hold on to the understanding of Christ expressed in the Scriptures and the confessions if he is going to be guided by the particular wisdom which comes from God. Unless the individual Christian believes, he or she will have no understanding—no wisdom which comes from God. Belief and wisdom are related in a very subtle but critical way. Without this perspective, even those who are wise by human standards will be doomed to living "under the sun." The despair and hopelessness of our times indicate that this is the experience of our day and times.

The mind of God is needed in the Halls of Wisdom, for we live in an age of increasing irrationality. Scripture needs to be looked at afresh.

The Scriptures are the guides for faith and practice.

They are not the guides for everything under the sun. The Scriptures contain a good deal about science, but the Scriptures are not a guide book for science. They tell much about ethics, but they are not a guide book for ethics. A great deal is said about philosophy in the Scriptures, but the Scriptures are not a textbook on philosophy.

The Scriptures tell us that we have one true and living God whose demands on us are absolute. They tell us that his help is sufficient. They keep reminding us that God is greater than our understanding and that we cannot fully understand who he is and how he works by human reason and that he reveals himself for his requirements are not always what human reason will lead us to think best. We are reminded in Scripture that God comes to us on his own terms and is able to do more than we think. There is no need to say, "there is no new thing under the sun." God can make us new creatures; he calls us to participate as partners in a new creation through Jesus Christ for Jesus's involvement in the human condition is God's involvement. The demands which Christ makes for truth, justice, and faithfulness are the demands of God.

If the writer of Ecclesiastes had not ignored the historical and theological traditions of Israel, he would have encountered the passionate conviction that God moves in history with people. The story of Israel along with the story of the church is the biblical record which tells how God has moved with Israel and the church toward the kingdom of God. We can thus see in this writer an example of the danger that is involved when we ignore the dimension of history. Faith then loses its recognition that God is moving toward a city without walls. The present is the frontier of that future. God keeps picking out from the past the things which are worthwhile to be used in the present, for the present must be kept faithful to the purpose of God.

This is our faith. It looks backward and forward to grasp God's dealings with us. But faith also comes from hearing and hearing comes from preaching. Thus, this faith is related to the Word of Christ. Without this Word, we inevitably become like the people of the Sage's day. We conclude that life is empty. Without it, and the perspective it gives on the future, we are in despair.

If we think we can find the true Good only in a wide knowledge of the practical aspects of getting along, of establishing ourselves, of understanding the social conditions of life, we will become cynics. Even if we pride ourselves in knowing people, in understanding their hopes and fears, their struggles and successes, their rights and wrongs, we will share the defeats of the Sage and end up crying his bitter cry, "Vanity of vanities, vanity of vanities, all is vanity." That is the way it is. You keep searching for a solution which you can never reach through wisdom under the sun because that kind of human wisdom keeps trying to make man the center of life when in reality God is the center of all meaningful dimensions of life—others, order, reciprocity.

Age after age, unwarned by the failure of those who took this road, we continue to renew the hopeless task of trying to build an anthropocentric theology, when God is calling us to a Christocentric theology. We begin our social action theology where man is rather than beginning where God is.

We thereby refuse to live by grace, under the lordship of Christ for the glory of God. Meaning well, with social improvements as the goal, we still go astray. The Sage describes this condition in his search for the best Good through wisdom. In this context, we realize that in a sense, the Sage affirms what God affirms. Even though he has a limited knowledge, he affirms that the world cannot be run successfully on the knowledge of man by man's plan.

The world must be run on God's plan. Yet we usually do

not find the mere statement of this fact to be sufficient without discussion. The Sage did not find it true. In his day there were too many programs put out which had no apparent regard for God's plan. The fact that they came to nothing in the end does not dissuade others from following the same road.

The fact that wisdom makes sufficiently clear is that every device must be run on the plan of its maker.

No one tries to run a wagon on the same plan as a cart, even though both are very simple machinery. A world must be run on the plan of its maker, just as surely as a wagon.

Institutions and nations are made on designs as definite in the mind of God as the automobile is made on a design which is definite in the mind of man. It is wise to use the steering wheel. God had a design for the nation Israel. God has a design for the United States of America.

For centuries men have been trying by their limited wisdom and knowledge of history and science to tell how nations came into being and how they should be managed. They draw their conclusions from a world which has been disfigured and distorted by sin. They live under the sun. The result is that the wisdom of one period becomes the foolishness of the next. The great temptation of Christ was to take the wisdom of the popular way–the Devil's way—to win the kingdom. The wisdom of people who live under the sun has not guided them to say "Get thee behind me."

Few nations of modern time seemed to have followed the false light of wisdom under the sun with more loyal devotion than did Germany up to the revolution of 1918. They took seriously the idea of "struggle" from Darwin and added to that the idea of "force" from Nietzsche. To this was added the idea of serving the fatherland. The culture of Germany which led up to the First World War was not different from the culture of France or Russia or other nations of the world, except that it was carried out with German thoroughness. The culture of Germany with German thoroughness followed the idea of "struggle" and "force" in the interest of the fatherland. Wisdom and reason dictated the course of action. God has not destined force to rule the world. The Kaiser's armies did not overrule the plan of God which calls for the rule of love in the world.

God affirms and vindicates himself again as he did with Waterloo. God did not make the world to run on the plan of Nietzsche. That is sufficient reason why it will never be run successfully on the plan of force.

Look back and examine the wrecks along the road of history. Did the Sage tell it like it is?

Look at Assyria, Babylon and Greece and Tyre. Why did these nations cease to have a place in the nations of the world? Why have their civilizations vanished sometimes without leaving a living trace? Why have the capitals of these nations, whose armies once ruled the world, become heaps of dust in which the spade of the archaeologist digs in order to uncover the palaces of the kings who aspired to rule the world by their wisdom? They had art and literature like the nations of our present times. They had their schools and their universities and their libraries. Paganism had an outstanding record in its material civilization and wisdom. The ships of Tyre sailed all the known seas. Egypt was a great empire—great in education. History tells us that Greek scholars went to Egypt for study. She was great in engineering, for the building of the pyramids is still a marvel of the age. There were times in the history when it seems that she might last like her pryamids. Bible history tells us that God vindicated himself by freeing the children of Israel. Secular history tells us that her civilization is as defunct as her mummied kings and queens.

Babylon was the wonder of the world and the marketplace of the nations. Her great monarch stood on the city wall, surveyed feats wrought out in palaces and hanging gardens and asked, "Is not this great Babylon that I have builded?" It was hard for him and people of wisdom of his day to understand the most high rules in the kingdom of men. The empire of Babylon was wrecked because people in their own wisdom tried to plan and work for their own salvation.

Look once more: We have Rome, the mistress of the world. She was considered to be so enduring in her character and so stable in her government that she was called the Eternal City. Historians tell us that Rome fell because of the coming of the Germans from the North. But Rome fell as the tree falls because it was rotten at the heart.

In the light of these wrecks and in the light of what the Sage tells us, we would do well to examine our own history since 1918 up to the present time.

Mueller, writing about Barth, says that

> One must recall that for Barth the prevailing school of the-
> ological liberalism lost much of its luster when ninety-three
> intellectuals, including some of Barth's theological teachers,
> signed a manifesto in August, 1914, supporting the Kaiser
> and the German war policy. Gradually but surely it became
> evident to Barth and Thurneysen that liberal theology had
> been weighed in the balance and found wanting. They gave
> themselves assiduously to the preparations of their sermons
> and serious biblical study, and published the first of several
> jointly authored sermon books in 1917 entitled *Seek God and
> You Shall Live* (*Karl Barth*, David L. Mueller, page 20).

Does our wisdom regarding society drive us to this conclusion?

I do not know that Barth came up with all the correct theological answers, but I do know that you have to reckon with a person who deals with God.

People come to human fulfillment within the limits set by God, not within the limits set by man so that apart from

God, it is impossible to find the chief good of people under the sun.

God is the God of love who expresses himself by creating. He creates others and builds a social order based on the practice of serving as a blessing to others. The good life thus depends on God, for he continues to add to human life and we see this in the miracle of reciprocity—a rule of mutual exchange.

If people are not creative in sowing, they will never reap. If they sow in emptiness, they will reap emptiness. If they scatter the seed of selfishness, they will reap the fruits of selfishness.

People often set limits for social action which include only the physical well-being of hurting people. We ought not to ignore this area of life, but we should also include the emotional and spiritual well-being of people.

If people ever deal with God, they will have to come to terms with the question of the Eighth Psalm which asks, "What is man . . . why is God mindful of him?" God has set a configuration for man of *others*, *order*, and *reciprocity*.

Real life is meeting God. From Abraham to Isaiah, Israel's faith was meeting with God, the great other—the creator. God's government, the people's loving allegiance, and the demand for decision were the issues that the people were called to face. God's love and the people's loving response were the source of power for community.

They were called to build an order of government and a community. These were to be built on loving God with all their being and loving their fellow human beings as themselves. They were to be built on the principle of reciprocity.

Life is a responsible activity in a living world. God has created us as expressions of life. We, too, are alive and we are sustained by the characteristic vitality of love of life itself. The demand for our commitment is direct and simple. We are called to surrender our inner consent to God.

Perhaps we can think of the ancient temple of Jerusalem as an illustration. From this perspective, the temple helps us to see the ways in which we gradually become a living expression of true life.

In this visual aid, the temple, we have in the outer court the altar of sacrifice. We are called upon to present all of our lower needs, our body, a living sacrifice to God through living on a spiritual level. We are created to live on this level and to discipline our lower needs for this purpose.

The yielding of the one nerve center is a private, personal act. The human being as sovereign says "yes" to God, the source of life.

The ability to say "yes" is not the result of any special talent or gift. It does not come from having any special status due to birth, social definition, race, or national origin. It does not depend upon wealth, sickness, health, creed, or absence of creed. The altar of sacrifice calls simply for surrendering our inner consent to God.

You now go into the holy place, where you come to the table of shewbread. This visual aid represents the bread of life. If the meaningfulness of the universe is characterized by the quality of life within it, we must realize that we truly begin to live by seeking a goal, called in Scripture the Kingdom of God. The world of God keeps this goal before us in wisdom that comes from above the sun. With this kind of wisdom you can deal with the temptations faced by Jesus in the Gospels. You can deal with the temptation to focus primarily on physical needs, the temptation of bread alone. You can reject the temptation of irresponsibility, of leaving everything to God. You can, as in the story of the gospel, avoid the temptation to cast yourself down from the temple and live under the sun. You can also deal with the third temptation, the allure of the ease of compromise.

In this temple illustration, the altar of incense is next. With its sweet-smelling savor going up to God representing the prayers of the people, who pray with Christ as he prayed in the garden, it expresses not my will but your will be done.

The next visual aid in the temple is the golden candlesticks which give a light to the world under the sun. This visual aid burns continually because a tube runs from the candlesticks to a reservoir filled with oil. The oil represents the Holy Spirit. When the conditions of surrender are met, the energy of life is available.

The next aid to our imagination is the holy of holies, the place in the temple where you find the ark of the presence. The life which is alive flows to and from the source of life in loving commitment that makes it possible for a person to yield the nerve center of his or her consent to a purpose or cause, a movement or an ideal, which may be more important than whether the body lives or dies, for the body has already been presented a living sacrifice to the source of life. As individuals we are alive in a more profound way than ever before. Our identity and relationship with God is affirmed and the energy of life continues to be available for us. We have actually come to terms with life.

It is well to remember that we are created to seek God and to live open to God, open to others, open to ourselves, and open to the world, for "we've a story to tell to the nations." This story is about the "Chief End of Man."

The Sage could not find the Chief Good in the realm of wisdom under the sun. He was wise enough to know that he had failed in his social experiment with the Chief Good as his personal goal and social goal, so he moves to another realm. Sometimes we do not realize that we have failed through the use of our limited wisdom. The Sage does, so he moves his search to the realm of pleasure.

Chapter 3
The Search
In the Realm of Pleasure
ECCLESIASTES 2:1–11

The Sage could not find the object of his quest in wisdom, so he turned to the other extreme and thought perhaps he could find it in the realm of pleasure.

We may want to travel this road, but the Sage tells us before we start that he has tried this experiment and he tried it on a grand and large scale. What can you do that the Sage did not do? I want you to know that the Sage had a good time.

When wisdom failed to satisfy the desires of his soul, he turned to mirth and once more he was disappointed in the results. He pronounces mirth a brief madness. Wisdom and pleasure are good, but to make either of them the Chief Good is to rob them of their natural charm.

You will not be satisfied with the Sage's conclusion. He knows this so he goes into spelling out the detail. Speaking in the person of Solomon and recounting the facts of his experiment, the Sage reminds us that he started his quest with the greatest advantage, for what can he do who comes after the king? He surrounded himself with all the comfort and luxury of an oriental prince. He did this not out of any vulgar desire for show and ostentation or sensual addiction.

He was objective in his experiment because he wanted to know the secret and fascination of pleasure. He built himself new and costly palaces. He laid out a garden and planted them with trees, vines, and fruit trees. He built reservoirs for water and constructed channels which carried the water to the roots of the trees. He bought men and women and surrounded himself with servants and slaves. He had indoor and outdoor slaves. He had his own private club and hired famous musicians, singers, and dancing girls. In addition, his harem was crowded with beautiful women from his own land and from foreign lands. He withheld nothing that his eyes desired and did not keep his heart from any pleasure. He set himself seriously and intelligently to make happiness his chief end while cheering his body with wine as he kept his senses about him all the time.

In our experience we also know some people who set out to have a good time with wine or other forms of alcoholic beverages. They overindulge and soon pass out and do not know what is going on. But they still say on the next day, "We surely had a good time last night." It seems that the Sage was more intelligent. He knows that if you rapidly gulp wine, it shocks your system and you pass out. The Sage was wise enough to sip his wine, so he kept his senses about him all of the time. Still, he says that his pleasure mocked him. The pleasure was empty and did not satisfy. When he had gone through the full career of pleasure and then turned to contemplate his delights and the labor they had cost him, he discovered that they were also vanity and a vexation of spirit. There was no profit in them. They could not satisfy the deep craving of his soul as a true and lasting Good.

The Sage had focused on the body and had forgotten the story of Genesis, which tells us that God created man's body and then breathed into it and man became a living soul. Man who is created by God as the high priest of the order of creation is made of the same substance as the animal and vegetable world, formed "of the dust of the ground." But his existence depends on the "breath of life" which he has only as the gift of God. The Sage with his optimistic humanism had focused on the body, rejecting the "breath of life" which comes only as a gift of God whom the Sage had ruled out by "living under the sun."

A materialistic philosophy which deals only with the body follows the same unrealistic course that the Sage followed in his search in the realm of pleasure. The focus is only on the physical and emotional sides of man's nature, and assumes that he is nothing more than an animal. Anyone who understands the Chief Good for man must see him in the totality of his nature with God as his creator as told by Genesis.

The sun as it seems may go on forever, but the sun cannot think God's thoughts after him. It can fulfill God's purpose, but it cannot exercise conscious choice to do so. Man alone can answer when God speaks to him, hear his law, and make or withhold his conscious and deliberate response. Man is a creature made in the image of God with the function to have dominion. This high privilege tempts him to forget that his dominion is delegated dominion. Man is lord of creation and ruler of nature not in his own right or to work his own will, for he is charged with working God's will and is responsible to God for his stewardship.

The Sage was trying to subdue the world for the pleasure of his own body and not for the glory of God. The Sage rejected delegated authority and, when he did, his pleasure was empty.

As Christians, we accept Christ but, in our understanding of God's revealing himself, we fail to deal seriously enough with the fact that Jesus Christ is the center of God's revelation and that we are members of Christ's body. Our pleasure sometimes does not reflect Christ as we try to cheer our bodies with wine or comfort our bodies with drugs. We do not know how to deal with the drug culture. We live a life apart from Christ and miss the revelation of God in our experiences with pleasure. In our day we experience the same emptiness that the Sage experienced, because with him we live without the revelation that comes from God.

After pronouncing wisdom and mirth vanities in which true Good is not found, the Sage does not move at once to a new experiment. He stops and compares these two vanities (Ecc. 2:12–23).

He prefers the vanity of wisdom over the vanity of pleasure. Neither one of these vanities, he decides, leads to the Chief Good, but if you are going to be a fool and live without God, it is better to live in the realm of wisdom than in the realm of pleasure. Wisdom is better than pleasure as light is better than darkness. It is better to have eyes that see the light than to be blind and walk in constant gloom. It is by the light of wisdom that he has learned of the vanity of pleasure. In fact, it is by the light of wisdom that he has learned of the insufficiency of wisdom itself. We have enough wisdom to split the atom and develop atomic energy, but we do not have enough wisdom to use this knowledge unselfishly. We are scared to death that someone will drop an atomic bomb and blow us all to emptiness or that industry will develop nuclear energy before being sure that it will not destroy us.

But for wisdom, the Sage might still be pursuing pleasures which do not satisfy or laboring hard to acquire a knowledge which would only bring more sadness and misery. Wisdom has helped him to understand that he must seek the Good which gives rest and peace in other areas of living. He no longer goes on his search in utter blindness. He has already learned that two large areas of life will not bring what he is seeking after. No longer does he need to

waste his brief day and failing energies in these two cate-
gories. Therefore, wisdom is better than pleasure as light is
better than darkness. Wisdom is better but it is not best. It
cannot remove the despair of the thoughtful heart. There
has got to be something better.

Wisdom cannot explain to him why the same fate comes
to the wise as to the fool. Wisdom does not help the anger
that keeps overtaking him when he sees the injustice that is
so obvious and flagrant.

Wisdom does not help him understand why the sage is
forgotten as quickly as the fool, for they both must die.

Wisdom does not help him get hatred out of his life which
has been caused by patent injustice. They tell him to prove
himself and justice will come. He knows that is a lie. How
can he believe any of the rulers or leaders of his country?

In this tangled world a man has no fair profit from his
labors. This thing bothers him all day long and even at night
his heart finds no rest. When he dies he loses all things he
gains, such as they are, forever. He cannot even be sure that
his heirs will be any the better at receiving what they can get
from him. This is bitter emptiness.

The Sage concludes that there is a wise and gracious
enjoyment of earthly delight. It is right that a man should
eat and drink and take a natural pleasure in his toils and
gains. Still, even this natural enjoyment is a gift of God. And
if eating and drinking becomes the ruling aim and chief
good of life, one finds that this, too, is vexation of spirit.

The Sage winds up on a negative note. The moral problem is still not solved. All we have learned is that wisdom and
pleasure will not lead to the end we seek.

Both wisdom and pleasure are good, but neither or both
combined is the Chief Good. We should acquire wisdom and
knowledge and have pleasure in our toils. We will do well to
believe that pleasure and wisdom are gifts from God and

that they are given by our creator according to the law of love. Yet we still have with us and in our hearts the baffling mystery of life. How do you find the Chief Good in a world among creatures who ignore their creator?

We write in our constitution that all men are created equal. We are aware of our creator and yet we go on ignoring him. How does a black person find the Chief Good in this kind of nation? Who tells him about the good news of God revealed in Christ?

The search must continue in our day and time. The word of God is the word that God spoke, speaks, and will speak in our midst to all men. Our God is the God who is, who was, and who will continue to come into the affairs of men. God speaks regardless of whether he is heard or not.

But let us go back to the Sage as he continues his search for the Chief Good.

Chapter 4
The Search for the Best Good
in the Affairs of Business
ECCLESIASTES 3:1–5:20

The Chief Good has not been found in the Halls of Wisdom nor in the Gardens of Pleasure. Perhaps it can be found in the market through devotion to business and public affairs. The Sage gives his efforts to this experiment. Immediately, however, he finds that he is in the hands of God's providence. He cannot get away from the fact that God is everywhere. No one can do anything anywhere apart from God, so the search is obstructed by divine ordinances. For instance, there is a time to be born and a time to die. A person does not determine the time of birth or the time of death. That is in the hand of the providence of God.

There is a time to plant and a time to pluck up what is planted. People do not determine the seasons of the year; that, too, is in the hand of the providence of God.

There is a time to laugh and a time to be sad. I do not determine the circumstances under which I laugh or the situation in which I am sad. These also are in the hand of the providence of God.

People go into business and exercise themselves in public life. Things do not work out as they have planned. They are distraught because they have no God to whom they can say "not my will but yours be done."

We believe that God provides for the needs of his creatures. This is one of our fundamental beliefs about God. In various ways God provides for the things and the people he has made, so that their existence can be maintained and continued. He provides life, rain, health, and other necessities for sustaining creation. His providence functions entirely independently of man.

We believe that God works in human history, but we live as if God has no part in our business or our economic or political affairs. Once in a while we will go to God and solicit his help, but in the main we live as though we are in control of economic life. This is what the Sage is describing in his experiment regarding devotion to business and public life without God.

If we do not find a satisfying Good in the events and affairs of life, it is not because we need to devise a better order of things, but because God has put eternity into our hearts, as well as time. We cannot be satisfied until we are working for Eternal Good. Eternal Good does not result from an organized business or political order. These things are the result of seeking first the Kingdom of God, where people work to glorify God and enjoy him forever, because we know that we live in the loving providence of God. Work against this providence, and life in business and politics will be empty.

God has ordained the regular cycle and order of events, as obscure as these might seem at times. Often they forestall the wish and efforts of the moment, leading us to discover that we should fear him instead of relying on ourselves. As Christians, we can place ourselves along beside the Sage and then, taking the perspective of the New Testament, and ask ourselves these questions:

1. Is Christ my Lord and Savior?
2. Do I trust Him?
3. Will I serve Him?

Can we answer *yes* to these questions in our political life and in our business life? If our answers are "no" to these questions, we will understand the thinking of the Sage, who thought that the providence of God was a hindrance to him in his search for the Chief Good in devotion to business.

As the Sage continued his search for the Chief Good in the affairs of men, he discovered that this search for the Chief Good under the sun was also obstructed by human injustice and perversity.

Not only is the good life impossible for godless people because of the inflexible laws of a just God, the good life is impossible because of the injustice of ungracious men. In the days of the Sage, iniquity sat in the seat of justice, breaking all of the rules of justice, for its own private, base, selfish ends. Unfair judges and rulers put the fair rewards of labor and skill and integrity in jeopardy. If people by the wise observance of divine laws and trusting providence had acquired money and influence, they were squeezed like a sponge by elite rulers, and their goods were taken from them. The poor people were punished by the rich, the powerful; the rulers were likely to escape punishment. They controlled the places of justice; one could not expect justice in the place of justice.

Understand the mood of the Sage by looking at justice in our own nation.

In his book, *Tell It Like It Is* (Trident Press, New York, 1968) Chuck Stone asks the question, "Who commits all the crimes in the United States?"

He answers by saying: "I don't know who commits all the crimes in America, but I know who most Americans believe commit most of the country's crimes—Negroes. Who else?"

Stone goes on to point out that we must examine a few facts about who commits most of the crimes in America. Where are the majority of crimes committed? Who controls the entire criminal network and syndicate in this country?

Stone quotes figures which show that, in the mid-1960s, the American cities with the highest crime rates were not the cities with the largest black populations. The top five were, in order, Las Vegas, Los Angeles, Miami, Phoenix, and Lexington, Kentucky.

The Federal Bureau of Investigation's report on crime in the U.S. for 1976 shows much the same thing. The cities of America with the highest crime rates were Las Vegas, Los Angeles, New York, Miami, San Francisco-Oakland, Detroit, Albuquerque, Daytona Beach, Orlando, and Memphis.

According to the 1970 U.S. Census, Las Vegas, with a population of over 270,000, has only 9 percent black residents. Washington, D.C., with a black population of over 70 percent, is not listed by the F.B.I. in a list of the top thirty cities with the highest crime rates. But included in the top thirty *are* such cities as Tucson, Arizona, and Yakima, Washington, and Stockton and Bakersfield, California—all with low percentages of black population.

Stone points out that Negroes control none of the organized crime in America. Individual Negroes are responsible for many auto thefts, but the control ring for disposal is white.

Prostitution in the major cities is controlled by whites. The ten most wanted criminals on the F. B. I. Wanted List rarely includes more than two blacks. The numbers rackets are also controlled by whites.

When you go to places of justice, that, too, is controlled by whites.

The Sage was not black, but I am sure he could understand the mood of Chuck Stone and Stone can understand the word of the Sage.

In the places of justice, the Sage expects justice, but there is no justice. He cannot find justice even in the place of righteousness.

In the first fifteen verses of the third chapter of Ecclesiastes, the Sage almost rises to a Christian height of patience, and resignation, and trust in the providence of God. But now he is struck with the injustice and oppression of man and falls into the pit of pessmistic materialism.

The Sage's survey of human life had lead him to think that there is nothing better for a man than a quiet content and a busy, cheerful, tranquil enjoyment of the fruits of his labor. He had thought that man could hope for at least this much. Now he begins to doubt that man can look for even this much when he sees the cruel way in which men deal with each other.

All of the activities of life are put in jeopardy by the providence of God through the inflexible ordinances of heaven, and added to these is the capricious tyranny of man. People groan under the heaviest kind of oppression. As he observes this scene of oppression, he doubts that contentment or even resignation can be expected of these miserable souls. There is no one who can say to them, "Comfort ye, comfort ye my people." There is no comfort for the oppressed and no comfort for the oppressor.

As the Sage considers their sad condition, he begins to think like Job in the days when his friends failed to bring comfort to his heart. The dead, he affirms, are happier than the living; even the dead who died so long ago that they are forgotten are better off than the people who have died recently. In fact, the people who are best off are the people who have never been born and seen the light of a day of a world all disordered and out of harmony.

In this kind of world, he begins to think that man is no better than a beast. A mere chance is man. The beast is also mere chance. Both spring from a mere accident. No one seems to understand how either one came to be in the world. There must be a blind creator, some unintelligent force at work. Both man and beast are subject to chance or mischance throughout all of their living. All of their decisions and intelligence and will are overruled by the decrees of an inevitable fate. Both man and beast are destroyed and suffer under the same power of death, suffer the same pangs of dissolution, and are taken unaware by the same invisible and resistless force. The bodies of both come from the same dust and return again into dust. In fact, both have the same spirit. Again the Book of Genesis is ignored. They fail to understand that God made man from the dust and breathed into him the breath of life. Forgetting this fact, the Sage concludes in this experience that one cannot prove whether the spirit of a man goes up or the spirit of a beast goes down. He is convinced absolutely that in origin, life, and death, in body, spirit, and final fate, man is as the beast and has no advantage over the beast.

If this is true, the Sage concludes that it will be smart for man to learn from the beast that simple, tranquil enjoyment of the good of the passing moment. One should not be troubled with the vexing problem of planning for the future. One should pay no attention to the God who keeps calling us out of the future into creative living. "Eat, drink, and be merry."

The Sage has gone off on a side road. The miserable lot of man has directed him from his main task of searching for the best good. He must return to his task. In Chapter 4, verse 4, he does return to the task. Now he argues that a person cannot get good fruit from a bad root. The task of finding the Good Life by devotion to business is rendered hopeless by the base origin of human industries.

Men go into the marketplace to find the Chief Good. The industries in which they work base their operation on man's jealous rivalry with his neighbor. Industry's operations have a base and evil origin. Every man tries to outdo and outsell his neighbor, to secure a larger business, to surround himself with more luxury, and to amass larger grouping of stocks and bonds. The business life is utterly selfish, and therefore utterly base.

People are not content with sufficient provisions for simple wants. We do not seek our neighbor's good. We have no noble or patriotic aim even though we may have "hunger" our chief priority. Our ruling intention in all of our work is to enrich ourselves at the expense of our neighbors, while their ruling intention is to enrich themselves at our expense. We become rivals rather than neighbors. People are trying to find their Chief Good at the expense of other people who are seeking their Chief Good in the same selfish way. Can we hope to find the True Good in a life whose aims are so sordid, whose motives are so selfish?

The sluggard who gets out of this rat race by folding his hands and doing nothing is better off than the fool who stays in and has a heart attack. (It should not surprise us if this were one reason welfare rolls were growing.)

The Sage concludes that the sluggard who folds his hands in indolence so long as he has bread to eat is a wiser man, for he has at least his "handful of quiet" and knows some little enjoyment of life, while the people who stay in this selfish rat race are driven on by jealous competition, eager cravings, and unfulfilled desires. They have neither leisure or appetite for enjoyment. They have both hands full, but there is no quiet in them. They are driven to labor and more labor and there is vexation of spirit.

The rivalry is so intense and selfish that the Sage is forced to paint a portrait for which no doubt many a person sat. It is the portrait of a miser, who is alone and kinless. He has no son or brother to inherit his possessions. Nevertheless, he hoards up money to the end of his life. There is no end to his labors. He can never be rich enough in his own eyes to allow himself any enjoyment of his gains.

Surely man is capable of a nobler way of living. Jealous rivalry ending up in mere avarice is surely not the wisest or noblest way to live. Men with good business minds ought to be able to find a nobler motive for living. Business, like wisdom or mirth, cannot be or contain the Supreme Good. Yet like wisdom and pleasure, business is not evil in itself. There must be a better motive for business than a selfish greedy one. The Sage begins to explore the areas of cooperation before he pursues his argument to a close. He begins to talk about union being better than isolation. Working together will bring a larger reward. To bring this suggestion home to the mind of the businessman, he uses five illustrations. Four of them would be clear to the oriental business mind.

The first is of the oriental businessman who has to travel. He says it is better for two to travel together than for one to travel alone. Travel requires going over a narrow mountain path. If one man travels alone, he could fall down the side of the mountain and break a leg. If he is alone, he could lay there and suffer and die for the lack of food and water. But if two are traveling together, the one could help the other up and get him to a source of help. It would be wise for two men in business to travel together. They should forget their jealous rivalry.

In the second illustration, the two travelers, tired from their day's journey, are ready for sleep. In that oriental country the days are hot and the nights are cool. The travelers wear long outer robes. If one traveler tries to sleep alone with his long robe to cover him, he will be cold. But if the two travelers sleep together, they would have to robes plus the heat from each other's body to keep them warm.

You see, the Bible is relevant here when it says don't let the sun go down on your wrath. Don't stay mad with your traveling partner when the sun goes down. You will freeze to death. It is better to have a little cooperation and sleep together. To sleep alone is to sleep shivering in the night air.

The third illustration is also taken from this oriental setting. The travelers are now sleeping well after their cooperation of walking and sleeping together. A thief comes in to rob them of their goods. If one man is sleeping alone, the thief can overcome him and take his goods, but if two men are sleeping together, the disturbance will awaken the other and the two together can overcome the thief.

The fourth illustration is that of a threefold cord. We, as well as the orientals, know that three cords twisted together are stronger than a single cord.

The fifth illustration is a great deal more elaborate. Again, we are back in the oriental East. You will recall from your understanding of oriental history that the tenure of royal power was extremely uncertain. Often a prisoner was led from the dungeon to a throne. A prince was suddenly taken from the throne and reduced to impotence and poverty. The Sage pictures such a case.

On the one hand we have an old king. He has lived and ruled a long time, but he is not respected for he has never learned to accept admonitions or advice. He has led a solitary, selfish, suspicious life. He has secluded himself in his harem, surrounded himself with troops, and lived by the flattery of his courtiers and slaves.

On the other hand, we have a poor but wise young man who likes people. He has lived with all sorts and conditions of men. He has acquainted himself with their habits, wants, desires, and needs.

The old selfish despotic mind is alarmed by his popularity and throws him in prison. His wrongs and sufferings make him one with a suffering people. So, by a sudden outbreak, the people rise up and, by a revolution of the kind that often sweeps through Eastern states, the young man is set free. He is led from prison to the throne, although at one time he was so poor no one ever gave him reverence.

This is the picture in the mind of the Sage as he tells it like it is. In these clear illustrations, the Sage sets forth the superiority of cooperation over the solitary, selfish life in business. Neighborly goodwill which leads people to combine their efforts for the Common Good is better than jealous rivalry which prompts people to take advantage of each other and to labor each for himself alone. Life could be better if people would cooperate for the Common Good.

But even as the Sage urges this better and happier way upon people engaged in business and public affairs and thinks about his illustration of the young man of social concerns led from prison to the throne, the old mood of despair comes back to him. Even this wise youth who wins the hearts of people for a time is soon forgotten. Even this, although it looks so hopeful, "is vanity and vexation of spirit."

God created us and placed us in the world. He has called us to unimpaired unity and unimpaired difference. He called us to live out our uniqueness in unity. This calls for something more than human efforts in cooperation. Anthropocentric theology will not bring the Good Life, only a Christocentric theology will result in the Supreme Good.

People-centered social action may bring us to organization for the Common Good. Only a Christ-centered social action will produce an organism which is working for the glory of God and which will live and not be forgotten. This is the conclusion which comes to light from the conclusion of the Sage. What conclusion can we draw from our own history and experience? Over against the Eastern experience, look at the Western experience. The Sage concludes that the more wisdom you have, the more sorrow you have; and the sorrow experienced in devotion to business could be better if people devoted to business would cooperate.

In Western experience, Protestant Huguenots were killed or expelled in France from 1685 until 1787. Many of them found refuge in America.

In England, the cities were filled with the degradation which was brought on by poverty, overcrowding, squalor, disease, and enforced idleness.

In Ireland, as in most of Europe, the peasants were forced to harvest more for the landowners than the soil could possibly produce. Surely all of the people felt that they were being squeezed as a sponge for the advantage of the powerful. The powerless in the West were treated the same as the powerless in the East. There was no one to comfort the powerless people or the powerful people.

Many of these unhappy people came to America. A cooperation in social living took place in America. This was an experience in social conscience which was unprecedented in the history of the world. When the thirteen colonies started their revolution in 1775, their leaders had only the vaguest notion of what kind of government would emerge once victory was won. Neither did the leaders and people know how they would deal with the perplexing social problems of the powerful and the powerless. These problems in the West are the same which the Sage faced in his day in the East. America, in this new experience which has always cherished the ideal, if not the reality, of equal opportunity for all, has respected and admired individual striving and accomplishments. Most of us have been taught to believe that industry, thrift, patience, and moderation are bound to bring rewards. We have been taught to develop an individual conscience which could lead us to believe in the survival of the fittest, unless our conscience is guided by the love which leads us to love God with all of our being and our fellow human beings as ourselves. We could believe the false doctrine that God helps those who help themselves. This is not the kind of God we know in Christ who calls us to a social conscience of community.

We do not know this God in America, but we do believe

that the American experiment is good. So through cooperation, which is better, we are trying earnestly to develop a social conscience. When illness or disaster struck the early settlers, the family and near neighbors came and pitched in to help, providing food, shelter, and financial aid. With the development of a more complicated society, communities began to recognize their responsibilities for the victims of misfortune and each town or parish took care of its own. People in this new experiment were determined to be noble.

After the Revolution, America entered a period of growth. The population grew; the frontier continued to move westward. New methods and machinery aided both industrial expansion and Southern agriculture. These changes caused immense changes in the quality of American life. Again we had to deal with the very powerful and the powerless. This situation called for moral and social stocktaking in our history. The movement that developed emphasized rights and aspirations of the individual. Leaders were people like Horace Mann, Horace Greeley, Ralph Waldo Emerson, and many others. I am sure that these social critics like the Sage were trying to tell it like it is in the hope of creating a better climate for cooperation through developing a social conscience which would guide us in living for the common good. God calls it the Kingdom of God—Community—but we cannot talk about the Kingdom of God so we talk about the common good.

Workers showed discontent, so they formed societies (really trade unions) for improvement toward the Common Good—"Best Good under the sun."

Women were often the most vocal and influential in this moral and social stocktaking. Women's own plight, their sketchy education, their ambiguous legal status, their uncertain role in a growing America—these were much on the minds of both male and female reformers. All of this was going on in 1848 when a bill of women's rights was adopted at a two-day convention in Seneca Falls, New York.

Of all the issues that claimed the minds of the reformers in this moral and social stocktaking, none was more important than the issue of slavery. Garrison developed *The Liberator* in the interest of the issue.

Charles G. Finney, a Presbyterian, turned his talent and prestige to Oberlin College in this effort.

Elijah P. Lovejoy, another Presbyterian, edited a Presbyterian paper advocating gradual emancipation. He was killed while defending his press from a mob in Alton, Illinois.

John Brown also lost his life for his attempt to spark slave insurrection in the South. Many others were involved in this movement.

Abraham Lincoln with a new party, the Republican Party, won the leadership of the country in an effort to deal with this issue.

The abolitionists had sought a dramatic change in America's treatment of her black people. Largely through their efforts, a war that at first was fought to restore the Union evolved into a crusade to free blacks from bondage.

After the Civil War the nation experienced the aftermath of reconstruction. The economic situation of the great mass of blacks remained bleak. They were powerless. Booker T. Washington through education, W. E. B. Dubois through the NAACP, and later the National Urban League tried to deal with this powerless life of blacks.

The years 1890–1910 are known as the Age of Reform, trying to deal with the life where those who are above are elevated and those who are below are crushed. Organized labor began to develop. But federal courts and state courts, influenced by the doctrine of Social Darwinism, took a dim view of much labor legislation. You are aware of the Sage's strong and clear statement that in the place of justice one cannot get justice, for the courts know little about social justice.

The country, however, tried to work at aiding the poor and helpless. All of this was done in a paternalistic fashion which left them powerless. Settlement works like the Hull House, started by Jane Addams in Chicago, were developed.

The farmers, like the urban workers, were poweless to deal as individuals with the problems of soaring transportation rates, low prices for their produce, and mounting costs for everything they needed. There was a farmer's revolt. The Populist Movement became an influential third party in U.S. history. Many of the reforms they advocated were later adopted by the two major parties. With the failure of the Populist Party, the progressive voice began to be heard in political reform. While Progressivism was not a successful movement, it did help to shift public opinion toward dramatic change which was soon to come.

Out of the Great Depression of 1929–1941 developed the New Deal under Franklin D. Roosevelt. He was greatly influenced by the Secretary of Labor, Frances Perkins, a noted social worker and the first woman cabinet member. Roosevelt tried to compel industry to social consciousness. The question was, and still is, can the necessary perspective and commitment be brought in order to maintain a growing social consciousness?

After the New Deal, there came the search for equality during the 1950s. This calls to mind the efforts of education, the NAACP, the Urban League, and the demonstration.

Problems grow and we come again to the equality of women, the crisis of hunger, and the crisis of energy.

By this time in the history of America, although headway has been made in the battle for improvement, the social evils of discrimination are still "moving us toward two cities: one black and one white—separate and unequal." We do not know how to deal with minority groups and the poor.

Lack of opportunity, unequal education and health care, unemployment, hunger, and slum living remain ugly realities of all who are willing to look. It is obvious that we still do not know how to answer the call of unimpaired unity and unimpaired difference. How do the powerful and the powerless learn to live together in unity for the common good? Is the common good enough or is that too vanity? Out of our experience can we come up with a different conclusion? Or did the Sage really tell it like it is?

The Sage was serious regarding his experience in cooperation just as we are serious about our efforts for social action and social conscience. He concludes, however, that the cooperation, even though it is better, it is not enough.

The Sage cannot get away from an idea planted deep in the soul. Even though he tries to live without God, he is still forced to believe that God works in human history. The text reminds us that the Sage knows that God has planted eternity in the human heart. There is no way to come to self-actualization and fulfillment in the political arena and economic life without dealing with the style of life which comes from bitter rivalries.

We live a style of life which causes hunger, causes farmers to be desperate because they get so little return for their efforts, causes miners not to be satisfied with their dangerous life. People keep trying to develop a social consciousness through fear and incentive. It seems to work for a while, but before long, things are like they were because the attitudes of people have not been changed.

In the providence of God, judgment keeps coming. The despair of the East is felt in a strong way in the West. Even though there has been an effort to develop a social consciousness, we are still faced with the desperation of farmers and miners. No one is saying, "Comfort ye, comfort ye my people." No one is saying, "not my will, but your will be done."

The people of the East had an opportunity to live in an abundant world. They had talents and abilities. God gave them the power of choice. They chose to live under the sun. We who are in the West also have an opportunity to live in a world of abundance. We have talents and abilities, too. We also have sufficient power of choice. We, too, have chosen to live without God.

We do not seem to remember that, fundamentally, we are characterized by the element of conscience, that we have the power of choice, and that we are obligated to live under the law of love. In spite of our efforts to find wisdom, the despair of the Sage of the East continued in the philosophers of the West.

The Sage of the East continues his search. He looks at an experience of worship in the church.

Chapter 5
A Better Way of Worship
Is Open to People
ECCLESIASTES 5:1

The Sage observed all the oppression and sadness throughout the earth. He saw the tears of the oppressed with no one helping them, while on the side of the oppressor were powerful allies. He had the feeling that the dead were better than the living. And most fortunate of all were those who had not been born and had never seen all of the crime and evil throughout the earth.

He observed that the basic motive for success is the driving force of envy and jealousy. This is foolishness—a chasing after the wind. Another piece of foolishness which he observed is a man who is all alone, without son or brother, yet who works hard to keep gaining more and more riches— and to whom will he leave it all? It is all so pointless and depressing even if he enters into cooperation through a social conscience to cooperate to make life better.

So the men of affairs are led from the vocation of the market and the pleasures of the couch to the house of God for worship. Surely in worship there is a better way of living. Our look at the worshipper does not give much hope, for here we find the men of affairs ready to offer sacrifices in place of obedience. They make repetitious prayers which

are long and run ahead of their weak thoughts and understanding. They quote the creeds but they have no idea what
they mean. They are quick to make vows regarding the
creeds and doctrine but they are slow to redeem the vows
which they have made. In the house of God, they deal the
same way they do in the marketplace. They bargin with God
as they do in the marketplace ("Get me out of this peril and
I will serve you"), but when the peril is over, they forget their
vows. The house of Worship is used like a launching pad—
to launch people into heaven so that, hopefully somewhere
between launching and arrival, they will learn to be obedient.
But while here on earth, they enter only to make sacrifices
while they do business as usual in the marketplace and make
the house of God a bargaining place of thieves who do not
intend to keep any vow they make to God.

The Sage wants the merchants and politicians to see that
they are the worshippers that he is describing. He tries to
hold up a mirror that they might see themselves as they are
and as others see them. They are the ones who vow and do
not pray. They are the ones who utter words that their hearts
do not prompt them to say. They take the road of sinning
and sacrificing for their own sin in lieu of obedience to the
Lord of the Church.

The people who give themselves in devotion to public
affairs do not often get much help and comfort from worship of God because they come to it with preoccupied hearts
and minds, just as people get little comfort from their beds
because their brain, jaded but yet excited by many cares, will
not let them sleep. People can not worship God because they
are preoccupied with the cares of their business. Other people have their minds back home in the oven with the roast,
afraid that it might burn before the long-winded minister
has finished his sermon. Young people are preoccupied with
the things which engage the minds of young people: Will

John be able to get the family car so we can drive out to the lake for a swim before youth meeting?

With the mind in this state, people often promise more than they can perform. They promise to serve God with all of their being, to love their neighbor as themselves. But they wind up being spiritual adolescents who think they can carry out their promise primarily through programs of evangelism and social action. Such people are often so preoccupied with their own individual salvation, expressed in the beguiling actions of good works, that they never realize that one cannot serve God without all of the inmost being and love. Both authentic faith and service are necessary, for we cannot serve God without facing up to righteousness, justice, and freedom in evangelism in action programs.

The Sage says, "I will show you a more excellent style of worship." Go to the house of God "with a straight foot"—a foot framed to walk in the path of obedience. Keep your heart, set a watch over it, lest it should be diverted from the simple and devout homage it should pay. Do not urge and press it to a false emotion, to a forced and insincere mood. Let your words be few and reverent when you speak to the Great King. Do not vow except under the compulsion of steadfast resolves, and pay your vows even to your own hurt when you make them.

There is no conflict between teaching the Word and living the Word. The teaching and doing is for the purpose of helping people to experience joyful obedience.

Thinking of ourselves in the West who profess the Christian faith, we do well to remember that the Reformation developed out of an effort to have a closer and more direct access to God. Leaders in this Reformed Faith were searching for the freedom from sin and systems which kept them from joyful and obedient faith in God.

These leaders developed a system of church government

through representative and delegated authority, for they believed that this arrangement would be most conducive to responsible faith and service.

Following in their steps, we will both talk and live the faith. We who vow to support and to live the Christian faith today will develop a humane system in which all people will have the opportunity to be unique creatures who are responsible for creation. There is no conflict between teaching, witnessing, living, and doing our faith in order that systems may aid people in exercising responsible freedom.

The Sage is saying we must not anger God and the angels of God with idle and unreal talk and actions by making vows which we cannot keep if we rule God out of our living and actions.

You know God is talking to us in the book in our times. When I read Ecclesiastes, I am not reading only of people long ago. This is me. This is my own society in action. I am part and parcel of that society. God is saying to me, "Don't be a phony by making vows you do not plan to keep."

Some people, in our day and because of our society, are beginning to call some evangelists "Magnificent Phonies." They are saying that, in this culture of instant coffee, instant tea, and instant cake mix, we are also trying to sell instant Christianity as a shortcut to heaven through messages which persuade people to make vows which they cannot keep. After the evangelist has moved to another town, people begin to try to diagnose why they got so excited and made vows which they find themselves unable to uphold.

People come to the evangelist weary with the cares of the world. But many evangelists may fail to deal with any of the specifics. Rather than coming to grips with the injustice and unrighteousness and oppression in the affairs of men, the evangelist says, "Take your burden to the Lord and leave it there."

We may not hear the evangelist saying, "Work out your own salvation, knowing that it is God who is working in you." No, we are not guided to deal with being human as unique creatures, responsible for creation in race, crime, unemployment, unequal education, inadequate housing, poverty, and dropouts in terms of the demands of Christ.

Sometimes the evangelist does not walk with Christ into the temple of God and guide us, both black and white, poor and rich, to break down the walls which divide us, saying to people who hold on to self-centered worship, "You are defiling the house of God with your denial of love and fellowship in worship."

So many people may ask the question, "What shall I do to inherit eternal life?"

We need to be aware with loving sensitivity that many people are seriously concerned when they ask this or a similarly phrased question. While this inquiry does not in itself express a mature Christian conviction, it is often asked out of a genuine longing for faith.

We can be led in our response to people by the dramatic scene in Chapter 6 of the Book of Revelation. In Revelation 6:9–11 we hear in the words of the author the cry of souls who are martyrs for God's word, "How long, sovereign Lord, holy and true?" While the two questions, that of the contemporary searcher and that of the faithful martyr, differ, there is an element of longing and hope that appears in both.

In answer to the question, the martyrs were given a white robe and were told to "rest a little longer." The robe is significant, for it represents God's gift of life and hope to us. In theological terms, it symbolizes the unmerited favor of God.

Comparable to his, the followers of Christ were asked, in the first chapters of Acts, to wait for God's gift of his Spirit. We are all brought to faith with both an assurance of eternal life and inner strength for keeping our vows by the gift of the Holy Spirit. God's gift of his presence is, in the graphic symbolism of the Book of Ecclesiastes, from beyond the sun.

God calls upon us to surrender to his love and to love him with all of our soul, strength, and mind, and to love our neighbor as ourselves.

In our society many people have the feeling that they have fallen among thieves. Many things have happened which cause them to think they are being robbed of their rights as persons. Ethnic minorities, women, the powerless, middle-aged white males, senior citizens. The strain and stress cause a real dilemma in our corporate life. God is saying to the worshipper, all of these people are your neighbors. Love them as you love yourselves.

In light of this situation and in light of the injunction from God and the vows we have made in response, the Sage would say, "You have not walked in worship with a 'straight foot.'" The Sage would say, "You are 'Magnificent Phonics.'" This is vanity.

The conditions of our society could be different if we would show in the exercise of worship a holy fear of the Almighty God. The Sage calls for keeping the vows we make in worship. As a result, the house of worship would become a sanctuary for all of the people who think they have fallen among thievery in society.

This counsel from the Sage is wise. Guided by it, we would move toward joyful obedience in both our actions and our worship. God's gift of his spirit thus undergirds and continually purifies the spirit of cooperation.

In his time, the Sage sensed that it was necessary for people to keep vows which are made in high moments of worship. It is important for us to understand that in making vows to God we always have to be on guard against authorities which are limited by attitudes under the sun.

Worship of God keeps reminding us that we are created

for living in a world of abundance. Worship of God keeps telling us that we have talents and abilities given by God. Worship of God keeps before us the challenge that we are created to live with purpose. It suggests that whenever we set goals, we should seek the Kingdom of God first. Worship of God also reminds us that we were created free—free to use the power of choice. The question is, What goals have we chosen?

This question is important for all aspects of our lives. The Sage goes on to show that when people returned from the house of worship to the common everyday tasks of the marketplace and were again exposed to the miseries of uncertainty of the market, they could be sustained and comforted if they would keep in mind that they could trust the divine providence. To the worship in spirit and truth in the place of worship, the Sage adds a strengthening trust in the providence of God.

As the Sage deals with this theme, the first fact of which he wants the people to be aware is that, even though there are oppression and injustice in the world, the judges and satraps who oppress them are not supreme. There is an official hierarchy in which superior watches over superior. If justice is not given by one, they can appeal to a higher official. If justice is not to be had from any—not even the king himself—there is the reassuring conviction that in the last resort, even the king is 'the servant of the field,' dependent on the wealth and the produce of the land, and can not afford to be unjust with impunity or push oppression too far, for fear he will decrease his revenue or depopulate his realm. This was the advantage that the people had. It might be but a slight advantage to one man alone, but to people acting in concert, it was a mighty weapon. It was of great advantage to the body politic. Men would do well to remember that in the providences of God, he ordained delegated authority. People can refuse to be slaves if they act in concert through the body politic and become servants who live in a democratic society—if they go from the worship of God remembering the providence of delegated authority.

The second fact that the Sage will have people think about and recognize in the gracious care of God is this: The unjust judge and the wealthy "lords" who oppress them do not find as much satisfaction in their fraudulent gains as the oppressed people might think. God has so made people that injustice and selfishness defeat their own end of finding happiness under the sun. Those who live for wealth and do evil to acquire it make poor bargains after all. He that loveth silver is never satisfied with silver. Nor is he that clings to wealth satisfied with what it yields. When riches increase they increase that which consume them—dependents, parasites, slaves flock around the man who rises to wealth and position. He cannot eat more or drink more than he did when he was just well-to-do in the world. He can only watch others consume what he has acquired at such great cost. He cannot know and enjoy the refreshing sleep of the farmer weary with toil.

He has to trust much to his servants and they might be unfaithful. Robbers may steal from him or his investments might fail. Officials might ruin him because of bribes they take from his sujbects or workers. If none of these evils befall him he may be apprehensive because he thinks that his heirs are waiting for him to die. He has nothing but vexation and grief. Why do we go around thinking that rich powerful people are happy?

In the providence of God oppressed people have a mighty weapon in their hands. They could let rich powerful people know that they know they are miserable and begin working for their salvation. Of course, if oppressed people have no God they can help the rich and powerful stew in their misery.

The Sage did not say that—I suppose he left that to the wisdom of the poor.

What the Sage did say is that even the captive or slave could find peace if his sleep were sweetened by his toil, and from his trust in God and the sacred delight of honest worship; this worship would give strength to endure all of the oppression of the time and enjoy innocent pleasures which came to him. If this were true, might not even he, the slave, be a wiser, happier man than the despot at whose pleasure he lived and served?

There are not many American businessmen who devote themselves solely or mainly to getting wisdom. Nor do we find many who give themselves exclusively to the pursuit of pleasure, although some may waste a little time in this area. But when the Hebrew Sage, after exploring wisdom and pleasure, enters the realm of business, which includes both commerce and politics, he enters a field of action and search with which nearly all of us are familiar. When the Sage tells it like it is in this area, he touches close to home for all of us. Whatever else we are, all of us are among the worshippers of the affairs of business. It seems that we all cannot help bowing down to the god "mammon."

Now as he deals with this broad and momentous area of human life, the Sage shows the candor and the temperance which he exhibited in his treatment of wisdom and mirth. He did not allow us to think of wisdom as evil in itself. Neither did he allow us to think of pleasure as evil. In the same manner, he will not allow us to think of business as evil. Business like wisdom and pleasure may be abused to our hurt. Abuse of these gifts from God is not his purpose for us. They are gifts to us from God to be used for our own good and for our neighbor's good.

If we can enter into business following the guidebook of God, working from the right motive with due moderation and reserve, business, besides bringing many advantages, could be a new bond of union and brotherhood. As we would follow the call of God to unimpaired unity and unimpaired difference, we would develop intercourse among people across lines of race, lines of sex, and lines of culture, which should develop sympathy, goodwill, and a mutual helpfulness.

On the other hand, if we refuse to follow the guidelines given by God, thrift may degenerate into miserliness and honest work and contentment may degenerate into a dishonest eagerness for an excessive worship of mammon. This kind of degeneration invites people to work for undue gains which may bring bitter results. So the Sage tries to warn us against excessive devotion to "mammon"—business.

The Sage handles the subject of excessive devotion to business with completeness and thoroughness. He tries to make clear that such devotion comes from "jealous rivalry" which tends to develop in people a grasping, covetous style of life which can never be satisfied. This style of life produces a materialistic skepticism of all that is noble, spiritual, and aspiring in thought and action. People will talk about noble thoughts being ideal, but they will conclude that they are not practical. Worship becomes formal and insincere. We talk about fellowship—and conclude it is ideal; fellowship is not practical when it comes to race, sex, class, and culture. Jealous competition results in formal, insincere worship which makes people totally unfit for any quiet, happy enjoyment of their life. This is the Sage's diagnosis of the disease called "our way of life" when we reject "God's way of life."

The Sage says that if we allow jealous competition to control our life, we will tend to become a covetous individual. As the Sage used his wisdom to examine the area of business, the facts of life made it impossible to deny that the eager successful conduct of business with excessive devotion tends to produce a grasping, covetous temper which can never be satisfied. It makes no matter how much you gain, you always want more.

You cannot get good fruit from a bad root. Or as it has been said another way, "The stream cannot rise above its source." "Not only is that true, it is also true the stream will run downward," someone else has said. As it runs downward, it will become polluted from things it picks up on the lower level. We may start out in business with noble thoughts, but as we follow the course of jealous competition, we will pick up the tendency to follow the spirit of covetousness and finally will forget all about the noble motives we had at first. In our experiences of working with young people we find ourselves with high hopes because of the noble thoughts of many young people, but we find that when they enter the adult world of business, something happens and they lose their noble ideals. They begin to adjust to the world of business and run downstream; they seem to forget that God, the creator, says "no" to jealous, selfish competition which will bring them to a dead end because God and all of nature say "no" to selfishness.

As the Sage tells it like it is, he points out that selfish people tend to form a covetous temper. Many observers are aware of the truth that the eager successful conduct of business and excessive devotion to business tend to produce a grasping, covetous style of life which is never satisfied, no matter how much has been gained. There is ever the desire for more and self-seeking is never completely satisfied.

People of politics and the business world often start out with high, noble motives, wishing to serve some public and worthy end or to bring about some change in culture and society, but the business person gets so absorbed in the pursuits of business that high motives and unselfish social change are forgotten. What is really wanted is more money and more glory, and there is no end to all of the labor and toil under the sun. Such people give blind devotion to their idols and think everybody ought to bow down and worship "their thing." People find themselves giving blind devotion to their idols—"their thing." This kind of action and thinking produces a close society of people built around certain idols of common concern. We become a people who are divided because we worship many different idols built around many different noble social concerns and business concerns. Materialistic, pragmatic skepticism is produced over all the places where we live, work, and play. Life is judged in terms of the marketplace. What will be gained from this action? What benefit is in this involvement to me? Before we know it, we are no better than beasts who are bent on protecting their own territory. Because people get accustomed to thinking mainly in terms of material interst, their character is materialized. Without realizing what they are doing, they are trying to worship God and mammon. When this happens, worship becomes formal and insincere. Worshippers who are devoted to this kind of materialistic living often become conspicuous by their absence or at best are noted for their occasional attendance; or if they do come regularly, they are preoccupied during worship with their business affairs. Such a life prevents people from experiencing any quiet enjoyment of life.

The Sage is making clear in this portion of the book that to live under the sun is to live on a material level alone. When life is lived on the material level alone, we have rejected God as sovereign in creation even though we do have noble motives for entering into business and social action. It is important to understand that God says "no" to the selfish use of any part of his creation. Try to use God's creation selfishly and you will come to a dead end—it is vanity—empty.

It is good to remember that God is sovereign and in con-

trol of history. He controls the physical world and the history
of nations, peoples, and individuals. God is also sovereign in
redemption. He puts no price on redemption, and we cannot deal with redemption in terms of the marketplace. We
do not bargain with God. God himself is present in redemption. He must be present in worship, for redemption and
worship are gifts of the Holy Spirit.

It is the sovereign power of God's love with which we
must deal as we live in the world. God leaves us free to say
"yes" to his love or to say "no" to his love. If we say "yes,"
God's wondrous love is seen in redemption. If we say "no,"
then his loud "no" of judgment is exemplified in our living.
God's judgment of "no" is made clear by the Sage in his
description of devotion to business and formal worship. God
has to say "no" to people who reject the sovereignty of God
by continuing to build walls of selfishness which divide us in
our economic, political, and social living. The judgment of
God brings us repeatedly to a dead end because he is sovereign in creation, in history, and in redemption.

The Sage experiences the sovereign "no" of God in all
the realms which he has explored so far because nothing is
changed in social relations unless attitudes are changed.

We cannot change attitudes by law. God reminds us of
this fact when we are told that it is not by power or might
"but by my spirit, says the Lord."

Transformation of the whole personality must take place.
We have heard it called "a new birth." The Sage sensed that
the new birth did not take place. The church experience
failed. So now the Sage turns to another realm as he continues to walk by his old nature under the sun.

We are forced to realize that people can advocate a correct faith and correct social action without having the spirit
and attitude of a relation of love which comes from faith in
God through Christ.

Since his church has not done its job of working for changed attitudes, the Sage seeks the Best Good, the Common Good, by dealing with wealth.

Chapter 6
The Search
in the Realm of Wealth
ECCLESIASTES 6–8:15

The Sage has seen that the Chief Good is not to be found in devotion to the affairs of business, as the Hebrew people of his time thought. This devotion to business was inspired by the desire to get great wealth for the sake of status and influence and as a means of having enjoyment. If they did not accumulate great wealth, they at least wanted enough to be comfortable. Selfish devotion to business led to a formal worship that was empty.

The question the Sage now asks is: Will wealth confer the good, tranquil, and enduring satisfaction which people seek?

The discussion regarding wealth is very brief. In the discussion regarding business some of the problems of wealth have been mentioned. In this sixth chapter, the Sage is dealing with the lover of riches. These people who love riches got a great deal of wealth. Immediately they learned what they were told about money in regard to devotion to business. When they got wealth, they discovered that they had more kinfolk than they realized they had and all these kinfolk wanted to live with them. This made them unhappy.

They also worried about losing their wealth. The stock

market might crash or someone might steal their wealth from them. They worried so much that they had stomach ulcers and the doctor put them on milk and crackers. They could no longer enjoy a big juicy steak. Other people could, and the rich were expected to pay for it. This made them extremely unhappy. More than that, they worried because they knew that at their death there would be a family fight over who would get the money.

The Sage says that the man who loves riches as his Chief Good is haunted by fears and perplexities. Remember that this chapter is dealing with the lover of riches—not with the rich person. The person who trusts in riches is placed before us. The Sage wants us to see him as he is and at his best.

God has given him "his good things." He has them to the full. But he does not accept his riches as a gift of God. Because he worships the gifts rather than the Giver, the lover of riches is unable to enjoy riches. He cannot trust God to take care of him and his riches, so he worries. He has not experienced the love of God, so he cannot share. He keeps building more barns to store up more grain, which is a symbol of his wealth. Meanwhile oppressed people in the world go hungry. God says "no" to this kind of selfish economic and political life. The lover of riches frets because he has no one to whom he can leave his wealth while there are hungry people all around him. The lover of riches frets because he thinks more of his wealth than he does of the God who gave him wealth and he thinks nothing of the opportunity he has to feed hungry people.

More than that, the Sage says the lover of riches is miserable because God has put eternity in his heart. The lover of riches does not seem to understand this truth, for "all the labor of this man is for his mouth"—his wealth, with all that it commands, appeals only to the sense and appetite. His wealth feeds the lust of the eye, the lust of the flesh, and the

pride of life. His soul, however, is not satisfied by the lust of
the flesh. The soul craves for food that wealth cannot pro-
vide. He knows without understanding that man does not
live by bread alone. He has got to do more than feed his
mouth. Because eternity is in his heart, man cannot be satisfied with the comfortable condition of time.

Look again at our money and possessions. We do not
really possess our possessions. They possess us. Multiply
them as we will, if we seek our chief good in them, they only
feed vanity and breed vexation of spirit. Once beyond a
certain point, we can neither use them nor enjoy them. We
can eat only so much food; we can wear only one suit at a
time. We can continue to add to our wealth and it will add
to our pomp, give us a larger place in the eyes of the world,
magnify the vain show in which we walk. But after all, to tell
it like it is, this love of wealth adds to our discomfort rather
than to our comfort.

We have more to manage and look after and because we
manage it in a self-centered manner out of jealousy and cut-
throat competition, we bring misery and suffering upon un-
told numbers of people who are manipulated into poverty
because of the selfish way we manage our wealth in order to
get more wealth for a vain show. We are unable to tell what
is good for ourselves. Everything turns out to be a bitter
disappointment and we cannot foresee what will become of
our gains.

Again, remember the Sage is not making an argument
against riches. His argument is against the undue love of
riches. He warns against loving them so much that we cannot
enjoy them while we have them nor trust them to the disposal
of God when we must leave them behind us.

If we can trust God to give to us all that will be good for
us through honest toil, we would be in a better position to
pay fair wages for honest toil to those who labor with us or

work for us. If we could have a firm trust in God, the warning of the Sage would bring hope and comfort. It would make no difference whether we are rich or poor. This kind of trust, however, is not a part of our daily life, we continue to live in a vain show with great anxiety in the midst of trouble and oppression. This is an evil which the Sage sees under the sun, and it lies heavy upon men.

Under conditions like these, the Sage decides to examine by wisdom the Realm of the Golden Means. He begins by saying "a good name is better than precious ointment."

In Chapter 7, we may begin to realize that only a few people get great wealth. There may be many who will say, "Who will show us any gold?" They mistake gold for their god or good. Although few may get wealth, there are many who crave for it and who think if they had it that they would possess the Supreme Good.

Because this feeling is both general and strong in the hearts of people, the Hebrew Sage gives himself to this issue at some length. He places before us the picture of a man who does not aim to get great wealth. This man makes it his aim to stand well with his neighbors. They will help him to build up moderate provisions for future needs and wants.

The man who takes this approach first tries to get a "good name." This "good name" would cause people to think well of him and open up money avenues which otherwise would be closed. In the oriental setting, which the Sage had in mind, if a man entered a crowded room with sweet ointment on his robe, a ready way was open for his approach. So the man with a good name would find it better than ointment for making a ready way for him in the crowded marketplace. He would find many ready to meet with him and do business with him.

How does a person acquire a good name? The superior Oriental moves with a dignified gravity and grace. He rarely smiles in public and almost never laughs and hardly ever expresses surprise. He must be cool, courteous, and self-possessed. If the news is good or if the news is bad, he keeps cool. Therefore, the man with a good name finds it better to be in the house of mourning than in the house of feasting. Serious thought is better than foolish mirth which crackles like thorns under a kettle, making a great sputter but soon burn out. Because he is determined to have a good name, he walks in the house of mourning and meditation. He does not harry with fools to the banquet.

We ask, "Why does he give up the pursuit of great wealth?" He answers that he has discovered wisdom to be as good as wealth, sometimes even better. "You see," he says, "wisdom gives an inner security that wealth does not give." "Wisdom fortifies the heart," while wealth often burdens and engulfs it—giving vexation of spirit. Wisdom braces the spirit for any new future, gives new life and new strength, inspires an inward peace which does not lie at the mercy of outward circumstances. Wisdom teaches a person to regard all the conditions of life as ordained and shaped by God. This kind of thinking helps him avoid vain endeavors so that he does not exhaust his strength on pomp and vain show as do the lovers of wealth.

All of this sounds pretty good. It looks like the man who takes this course is beginning to recognize the sovereignty of God when he says both evil and good come from God. Observe, however, what is happening to him. The theory of human life projected in this course of action appears good to us; our sympathies go with the man who seeks to acquire a good name as he endeavors to walk in the path of the wise. But when be begins to apply his standard of the Golden Means and to deduce practical rules from it, we begin to have some doubts and must often withhold giving our assent. He begins to draw the conclusion that you should avoid excess, that you should keep the happy medium between intemperance and indifference.

The people following the course of the happy medium draw conclusions which raise serious objections. They have seen the righteous die in their righteousness without receiving any reward from it. They have seen the wicked live long in their wickedness to enjoy their ill-gotten gains which they got through oppression and the selfish use of power. People have seen so much of this that they conclude that the prudent man will not be too righteous since he will gain nothing from it and may lose the friendship of those who are satisfied and content with the current morality. Neither will the prudent man be very wicked, since, though he may lose little by this way of life so long as he lives, he will very surely hasten death and come to death. He does not want to lose his soul even though he rejects the God who breathed into him the breath of life which made him a living soul. It is the part of prudence to hold on to both—do not be too good and do not be too bad.

Such people are like the people who worshipped in the Church of Laodicea. They are neither hot nor cold and God spews them out of his mouth because they are lukewarm. These are the people who compromise conscience. They remark, "I am not an angel but I am not a devil either." They are right. The hypocrites—they are nothing—they live on the fence. They do not like themselves and no one else is able to like or trust them. The moral is lay one hand on righteousness and another on wickedness and not much harm will come to us. This is a right immoral moral, but it is as popular in our day as it was in the day and times of the Hebrew Sage.

The next rule that the Sage sees developed by those who follow the road of the Golden Means as the Chief Good is: Do not get too concerned and overmuch worked up and troubled by what people say about you. Servants are taken as an illustration, for, like the Negro slave and Negro servant, they know and hear a great deal about the people they serve. The people being served do not know very much about the people who serve them.

Servants know a great deal about their master's faults and they do talk and sometimes they even exaggerate. "Let them talk" is the advice of the speaker of the Golden Means, and do not be too curious to know what they are saying. We may be fairly sure that they are saying pretty much what we often say about neighbors or superiors. If they are talking about us, we have talked about others. We can hardly expect to be treated better than we have treated others.

Perhaps if this moral stood alone, it would be both shrewd and wholesome for society. But it does not stand alone, and, looked at in connection with society, it means that if we take the moderate course as prescribed by modern society on her wisdom or prudence and become righteous without being too righteous and wicked without being too wicked, we are going to create a mess in our society. Our neighbors will begin to say, "Boy! I could tell a story about him. He is not as good as he seems." But we are not too concerned too much about our neighbor's story on us because we, too, can tell a story on our neighbor. We know our neighbor's secret. We conclude that there is not a righteous person on earth who is good and does not sin. In short, we are not to be too hard on ourselves for sinning nor become vexed by the censures which our neighbors give for they are as guilty as we are. Taken in this connected sense with our society, the moral is immoral because we are tempted to despise censure and excuse ourselves by saying, "Well, nobody is perfect."

The Sage is not satisfied with this excuse, this theory. He wants a higher principle by which to live. He keeps thinking there must be a higher wisdom—surely there is a nobler

theory of life than this. But it is too far away for him to reach
by human wisdom. After all of his research, that which was
far off remains far off. He cannot attain the higher wisdom
he seeks. So he falls back on the human wisdom which he
has tried before and draws a third moral. This moral is
practiced in our own enlightened society.

The third moral principle permitted society to despise
the personhood of women. The society built by male elitism
allowed men to depersonalize women for the glory of men.
Men use the bodies of women for their own selfish gratifi-
cation. This kind of society did not come from wisdom from
above. This treatment of women came from wisdom from
below. It was devilish and sinful.

Listen to the Sage describe the condition of the women
of his day. "I turned my mind to know and search out and
to seek wisdom and the sum of things and to know wickedness of folly and the foolishness which is madness." As the
Sage used wisdom and added up the sum of his research,
he says, "And I found more better than death the woman
whose heart is snares and nets, and whose hands are fetters;
he who pleases God escapes her but the sinner is taken by
her." Behold, this is what I found, says the Sage, adding one
thing to another to find the sum, which my mind has sought
repeatedly, but I have found one man among a thousand,
but a woman among all of these I have not found. Behold
this alone I found, that God made man upright, but they
have sought out many evil devices.

It would seem that society had concluded that woman
was the cause of sin and the way to deal with this evil was to
depersonalize her so that she could be converted to glorify
the male ego and serve man. At one time it was said that
black people were heathen, so God brought them into slavery so that white people could convert them to be good slaves
for the white ego.

This is a devilish, immoral principle upon which to build a society and style of life. Yet this principle has become so fixed in society that, today in our time, women are trying to build a moral society by becoming equal with immoral men who are responsible for building a society upon an immoral principle. Black people are trying to become equal with immoral white people who are responsible for building a society of immoral worship, education, politics, and economic style of life developed around cut-throat competition.

Examine the theory of the Sage thoroughly, for he did not draw a hasty conclusion. The Hebrew cynic had deliberately gone out with the lantern of his wisdom in his hands to search for an honest man and an honest woman. He was thorough and scrupulously careful in his search. He took things one by one and added them up and, though he found one honest man, it was impossible to find an honest woman. Was not the fault in the eyes of the beholder rather than in faces of the women at whom he looked? When men say that women are not called to be ministers, it is not the fault in the eyes of the beholder. God looks on the heart. What does he see in the hearts of men who have robbed women of personhood and natural dignity? Has he condemned them to be mere toys, trained only to minister to the flesh? What does God see in the hearts of men who say that women should not be called to the teaching ministry to minister to the spirits of people and teach them to be disciples of Christ? Of all the cowardly acts of the human race, denying women this opportunity is the meanest. It would be good for women to remember that it is not smart to be equal with men who are that mean. It would also serve blacks to remember that if people are mean enough to enslave them and cause them to lose their natural dignity, it is not smart to be equal with them. You cannot build a moral society by building on immoral principles thought up by the wisdom of immoral people.

Remember God made man upright—man as in Genesis stands for the whole human race, male and female, black and white, rich and poor. If human beings have degraded themselves and one another, it is because they keep seeking evil "devices" as they endeavor to find the "Supreme Good" by living "under the sun." Without God, oppressed people seem to want to live in the image of their oppressor. They strive hard to be equal with the oppressor. They want a good name so badly that they forget that they are created in the image of God. They will either submit to oppression or they want to be equal with the oppressor.

The fourth rule inferred by this prudent, moderate compromise vein of life is that we are to submit with hopeful resignation to oppressions and wrongs which come from human tyranny and injustice. The wise, temperate man in this oriental setting conducted himself calmly and carried a bright, shining countenance in the presence of the king. Even though the king would treat him in an evil manner, he would not get angry or express resentment. He would never think of open revolt. He knew that the king had power and that a hot temper would bring the power of the king down upon his head with wrath and that this would damage his cause. He reasoned that if a man would keep himself cool and not permit anger to blind him, the time of retribution would surely come on the king or the satrap who is habitually unjust; that the people would eventually revolt because of the wrongs done to them. The people believe in delayed justice, therefore they will not allow resentment to carry them into a dangerous course. They will calmly wait for the action of those social laws which will cause every man to reap the just rewards of his deeds. They do not talk to the oppressor about the laws of God—the oppressed people do not witness to the oppressor regarding the rule of God in the affairs of man. The oppressed people are indifferent to public wrongs being caused by the rejection of delegated

authority from God. They are indifferent to the salvation of
the oppressor; they hope for his destruction through social
laws which come from the wisdom of man. They are indifferent to Public Corporate righteousness.

As the Sage watches this way of life on the human level,
he observes that there are times when the social laws of man
do not catch up with the oppressor; retribution does not
overtake the oppressor. They rule on and on, even their
children follow them in oppression and the memory of righteousness seems to vanish from the earth. Wicked men seem
to live on in their wickedness. People take their ease in Zion
and remain indifferent to public wrong.

In our day, things have not changed in basic philosophy.
People of the church listen in the World Council of Churches
in Nairobi and they hear the same cry that no doubt came
from people in the day of the Sage.

The Honorable Michael Manley, Prime Minister of Ja-
maica, said to the World Council, "Liberation is about victims. Every weak nation exploited by a strong nation is a
victim. Every man and woman deprived of a chance to acquire the skills of our technological age is a victim." He went
on to remind us that every family that is undernourished is
a victim. People who are underpaid are victims. Manley expressed the idea that the spirit of our times is that of the
strong squeezing the weak like a sponge for the advantage
of the strong.

The process of trying to find the Best Good under the
sun continues. People who spend a lifetime at work and have
never once been asked to help plan next year's production
are still hoping that something can be done about the search
for the Common Good. They want to experience self-actualization and fulfillment. They want an opportunity to
exercise their power of choice and their talents and abilities
in this world which God created for the purpose of abundant

living. The Good Life was not being experienced because wealth and a good name were the goals of life.

This is the kind of condition the Sage was describing in his day. And he says because everybody was so busy seeking a good name, oppressor and oppressed alike, the result was indifference to public wrong. The people in Zion heard, but they were indifferent, taking their ease in Zion and world of public affairs. They could hear no one saying, "Comfort ye, comfort ye my people."

The Sage, therefore, in verses 14 and 15 of Chapter 8, condemns the theory of life where people make wealth and a good name their Chief Good for it causes them to compromise conscience, to be indifferent to censure, despise women, and become indifferent to public wrongs. This is no way to deal with human life and people created in the image of God.

Chapter 7
The Sage
Rechecks His Experiments
ECCLESIASTES 8:10–10

The goal of the Sage was not attained, so he continues his search. There is no other area in which he can look so he checks his experiment again. He must have made a mistake somewhere in his experiment for surely people can find their Chief Good under the sun; that is the only practical pragmatic way to live. To talk about God and love is ideal but it is not practical.

In Chapters 8, 9, and 10 the Sage tries to be sure that his conclusions are correct. He is sure that people will be hankering after their old errors. He has found the Chief Good but he had better be sure of his facts before he starts talking to hard-headed businessmen.

Beginning at the 16th verse of Chapter 8, the Sage begins to examine again his experiment in the area of wisdom. As yet he does not carry the understanding lamp of revelation, only the light of wisdom that comes from wisdom of time and space. For the present he will trust to reason and experiences and state the conclusions to which reason and experiences bring him. Reason and experience can do much for man, but they can do nothing about the moral problems which afflict his heart, the problem which he must solve before he can have peace. He tries many social experiments and thinks he has made progress and solved the mysteries of divine providence; the illusion will soon pass and the un-solved mystery of moral responsibility reappears. The busi-ness person does much in business by reason. Progress is made and such a person moves up the ladder of success. However, that person still has feelings and family situations which cannot be left out of life, so he or she experiences depression because failure is experienced in these areas. The moral area of an I-Thou relationship must be experienced. Conditions caused by the selfish use of wisdom are still as dark as they have always been. Man fails also because he is not able to see the future. Man cannot know the works of God in the future unless God reveals it to him through faith. God has planted eternity in his heart, but he looks only at time and space. Again he sees the proof of the failure of wisdom because the same fate overtakes the wise and the fool alike. In the end they both die. To the mere human mind life remains a mystery and death is a mystery still more cruel and hard to understand. The experiment checked out the same way it did the first time.

Now he must recheck his experiment in pleasure (Eccle-siastes 9:7–12). This experiment checks out also as it did the first time around. Despite his best efforts to have a good time while guiding himself with wisdom, his life is still not tran-quil. Man in this area has followed the philosophy which says whatever you can get, get; whatever you can do, do. We are on the road to the grave when there is no work or device; for this reason our journey should be a fun journey. Eat, drink, and be merry. At any moment all of this might be taken away from us. He still concluded that his pleasures mock him.

When he turns to recheck the realm of devotion to the affairs of the marketplace, he finds that these rewards are not good either. It checks out that his first conclusions were correct (9:13–10:20).

He tells a story to make his point. He tells of a poor man who was an expert strategist living in a little city with only a few inhabitants. A great king came up against the city with all of his lofty military knowledge to assault and take it, but the little poor man outwitted the military might and saved the city. Wise as he was, his wisdom did not bring him bread—no one remembered that same poor man even though the city was so small that all the people saw him daily. People were so selfish in business that they did not remember this poor man, even though by saving the city he made it possible for them to continue in business—cut-throat jealous competition is just that evil. A poor man's wisdom is despised even by those who profit by it. (Many a white person profited by the wisdom of Carver with the peanut, yet they despised him because he was a poor black man.)

The fool is of great power in the world, especially the fool who is wise in his own conceit and thinks that he belongs to a superior race. He may be insignificant in himself, yet he can do much harm and destroy much good. He makes the sweet ointment of humanity to stink by infusing it with his own selfish folly. He causes people to disrespect humanity which they should honor because that humanity was made in the image of God and is sweet. If the eyes of the fool were in his head, he would know this, but instead he has eyes that have no recognition in them, knowing neither himself nor others. That's what jealous cut-throat competition will do to the people created in the image of God. The people devoted to business in this manner do not recognize themselves as persons. Neither do they recognize other people as persons. The Sage has seen people who are as foolish as this raised to high places while people of noble spirits are degraded.

This situation continues; no one wants to try to dethrone

a foolish despot. We try to dig a pit for him and we may fall
into it ourselves, or if we try to break down a wall a snake
might be hiding in the crannies and bite us. We fear losing
our good names in society so we ignore our conscience; we
compromise and lose our respect for humanity. We may not
have much, but we are certainly not going to risk losing our
jobs. We learn to ignore public wrongs and begin to despise
the dignity of man along with the selfish despot of business
and the selfish despot of wealth. We, like the Sage, keep
trying to deal with the problem without understanding the
problem of man.

People keep trying over and over again to build a better
society and they keep finding that man is a problem to himself. Man has always been a problem to himself because he
does not fully understand where he belongs in creation. We
keep trying to build a good society and the people who are
trying to build the good society are themselves the problem.
People want to build a great society; they feel called to rule
and subdue the earth but are unable to understand the mystery of their being. They are caught in a dilemma which they
see to be tragic. But, like the Sage, they keep trying for a
better way of life.

At this point it would have been good if the Sage had
been able to turn to the Fifty-first Psalm. This Psalm is the
human cry of failure which causes despair—depression which
comes because one examines life and feels with the Sage that
it is empty. The Sage senses failure; the Psalmist senses sin
and grace. This grace is expressed in the Eighth Psalm. The
Psalmist senses despair and failure. However, the Psalmist
does not look at failure out of fear. He looks at failure out
of curiosity and turns despair into trust and faith. The
Psalmist knows forgiving, accepting grace which comes from
above. He has the faith to get up and try walking again after
falling. Since the Sage does not know the possibilities of

grace, he finds that his sin keeps destroying him and pressing him down. He realizes that the knowledge of the results of sin kept bringing unrest and torment. There is something wrong inside the Sage, but he does not understand that he is unclean and that he needs forgiveness.

In light of the Psalms, it is possible to have another insight as we look at the pit and the wall which the Sage calls to our attention. The Sage did not experience guilt because he did not know he was a sinner. He had ruled out of his life the idea of creation and the possibility of faith and vision. Wisdom, confined to time and space, taught him that he might work hard to change things in society by digging a pit for the person who was using power to oppress people.

The Sage did not understand that creaturely existence is good because it is created and blessed by God, but no aspect of creaturely existence is to be sought and depended upon as the Ultimate Good. Human existence as created by God is personal and relational. God loves each individual. He loves the oppressor, too. We cannot dig a pit for the oppressor whom God loves and try to change the social situation through revolution by taking power unto ourselves. When the social situation is changed and we take power for ourselves, we fall into the same pit we have prepared for the wicked despot. We never realize that we, too, were brought to birth in iniquity. When any aspect of human existence is made the ultimate good, it brings us to the pit.

Through revolution the Sage might overthrow the oppressor—an oppressive way of life, dictated by those in power, might be changed by taking power on one's own. And then a man will discover that the old serpent of power is hiding in the crevices of his own heart. The poison of selfish power is in his own blood stream and he fails to take the responsibility for freedon in the structure he builds for governing people.

What is man that God remembers him? With the Sage, we too fail to ask this question of the Psalmist. We fail to realize that human existence, created and willed by God, is the integration of reason, feeling, and volition through faith that leads us to be free and responsible in teaching transgressors the way that leads to God.

When we observe life we realize that we do not seem to understand the way of God any better than the Sage, even though we have Christ. Unfortunately, in time we experience with the Sage our own personal hell of the failures of wisdom, pleasure, devotion to business, wealth, the practice of the golden mean, and emptiness of worship. Examine the way the human race keeps experiencing failure. Why do we continue our efforts to live "under the sun"?

Remember that the Sage was investigating reality in relation to a future where the Supreme Good would be found "under the sun." He was looking at the structure of society as organized by man, observing the totality of all the forms constituting human social life. Man is the organizer of society, so we cannot look at society without also looking at what man is, what he believes. The basic convictions and attitudes of man are decisive and significant for they determine what our community is going to be like and what our churches are going to be like. The Sage knows this; he deals with this reality.

In talking about life "under the sun," leaving God out of the organization of society, the Sage knows that he is talking about man's faith in his power to redeem himself. The Sage does not consider himself or the organizers of the structure of his day rebels against God, because they had ruled God out of their institutions. In light of what we know about the lordship of Christ today, we know better, but the Sage was not dealing with the reality of revelation. He was dealing only with the reality of human wisdom.

The Sage had the spirit of the offended Jew, the wise Greek, the aristocratic Roman, the hardened humanist, the perplexed Pharoah and, in some respect, he even antici- pated Nietzsche. The Sage, with these people, had the spirit of self-maintenance and self-redemption. Redemption through being children of God was a source of mirth or an object of scorn.

The Sage used human wisdom to indulge in speculation about utopias, with the result that he confesses to shameless cynicism and fatalism. The Sage, like all the builders of uto- pias, was driven by home-sickness for the paradise which was lost by living "under the sun." His dream was never realized because he walked a road to the Supreme Good which did not deal with the pervasive power of sin. People, in all ages, like the Sage, keep testing the same theory.

The "Republic" of Plato was such an effort. Plato's object was to construct a theory of justice. His practical wisdom led him to believe that "justice" implies that the just man is happy and that happiness is profitable and useful. It was his thinking that justice was best obtained on a large scale, so he developed his theory of the state in an effort of self-salvation.

People keep searching for the ideal society, so Thomas More, who lived in the period 1478–1535, wrote about his idea of the good society. In the year 1516 he gave people his vision of the ideal society in a work called *Utopia*.

More is described as an English humanist who with Er- asmus was the most important representative of humanism in Northern Europe. This does not imply that More was not a Christian. The humanism of that period had not yet bro- ken with Christianity. More only had the seeds of ideas that were later to lead humanism along an unbiblical course which more and more separated it from Christianity.

More was a steadfast and pious Roman Catholic. He was knighted and held in high esteem as Lord Chancellor of

England. He was untainted by the corrupt practices of his time. His written ideas reflect the attitude of the existing humanism.

People lived in a society where authority was exercised by ordering and demanding. Henry VIII was king. More refused to acknowledge the forced break of the king with the Catholic Church and Parliament's coerced proclamation that Henry VIII was head of the English Church. For his convictions, More lost his life.

In the first part of *Utopia*, More criticizes the society of his day. The second part is a vision of his ideal society. He wanted social justice. He thought it could be legally enforced through a central organization. He gave no thought to personal action according to the command of love. He thought the good society would come under the authority of ordering and demanding. Freedom and responsibility did not seem to be a part of his thinking in his period of history.

More criticized the society of his day and tried to correct it by building a society that also abolished private ownership. He differed with Plato, however, in that he kept the family

There have been efforts of self-determination down to our own day. Give attention to Huxley's *Brave New World*, published in 1932. Already, however, we think about "The New Deal," "The Fair Deal," "The Great Society." We think of the disappointment of all these efforts and we understand something of the flavor of the Sage's investigations "under the sun." The truth of the Sage is that he finally realizes there is no hope for the "Supreme Good" "under the sun."

Chapter 8
The Quest Achieved
ECCLESIASTES 11

The Chief Good is not to be found in wisdom, nor pleasure, not in devotion to business—the affairs of men and their rewards—but in a wise use and a wise enjoyment of the present life combined with a steadfast faith in the life to come. Chapters 11 and 12 in Ecclesiastes help us to see what the Sage is saying after he sharpens the ax. He had reminded us earlier that if the ax is dull, we have to use more strength. He has now sharpened his ax of wisdom with some wisdom from above.

Human beings seem to have a strong desire to absolutize human reason. When this is done, human effort results in emptiness. Perhaps we need to learn that when we absolutize reason, we are just as unfulfilled as the sentimentalists who absolutize feelings at the expense of reason. People who absolutize either indulgent feeling or reason must listen not only to the Sage, but also to Isaiah who says, "The whole head is sick, and the whole heart faint. From the sole of the foot even to the head there is no soundness in it, but bruises and sores and bleeding wounds; they are not pressed out, or bound up, or softened with oil."

We put insane people who are dangerous to society as well as to themselves in institutions so they will not hurt others. However, those who are aliens from true life because they have absolutized reason or feeling, we leave free to go on hurting each other. Paradoxically, they may in the end cause the greater hurt. Protesting innocence, they continue to be a people ladened with iniquity, offsprings of evildoers. Claiming virtue after virtue, they become the sons who deal corruptly. Despite the worldly pleasures, they have lost their capacity for true joy. They have forsaken the Lord. They have despised the Holy One of Israel. They are utterly estranged.

Yet the God they forget in truth is aware that they even come to worship with empty hearts. God asks of these sick people, "Who requires of you this trampling of my courts?" He says to them, "Bring no more vain offerings; incense is an abomination to me." Knowing the truth of our wilfulness, he is, however, a God of love and continues to reach out for all of us sick people, saying, "Come now, let us reason together . . . though your sins are like scarlet, they shall be as white as snow; though they are red like crimson, they shall be like wool. If you are willing and obedient, you shall eat the good of the land, but if you refuse and rebel, you shall be devoured by the sword; for the mouth of the LORD has spoken."

The Sage senses this great truth. Man cannot reason alone. He must reason with the God of love who says, "Come now, let us reason together." Human beings are created to live in a loving personal relationship with a personal living God. The Sage realizes now that human beings cannot live under the sun and find the Chief Good.

What that Good is and where it may be found, the Sage now proceeds to show. Being true to his nature and manner, the Sage does not say in so many words, "This is the Chief Good of man" or "You will find it in this place or that place." Instead he sets before us the man who is walking in the right path and drawing closer and closer to it. Following what seems to be his favorite method, the Sage gives us some maxims and counsel. From these we can understand who succeeds in the quest for the Best Good. He is not the man who lives under the sun by human reason alone.

At the outset, we see that the happy man is the one who knows the love which comes from above the sun—a love which comes out of the mind of God. "Cast your bread upon the waters." In the East bread was made in thin flat cakes. If it were thrown upon the water, it would disappear and yield no return. The love that comes from God guides the individual to give, looking for nothing in return. This is the love of God which is so great for the world that he gave his only son without price. We learn that the happy person is touched by this love and then develops a noble, unselfish, generous disposition. The happy person is not like man who simply wants to get on in life and make a fortune. The people who are finding the Chief Good do not grudge other people their gains. They look to their neighbor's interest as well as their own, and they will do good even to the evil and unthankful. They cast their bread on the waters and they will give a portion to seven, even to eight. The happy person knows how to show kindness which will be forgotten. It will never be returned, yet he is not dismayed by the thanklessness of the task. It may seem thankless but it is not, for the good of it is found in the loftier, more generous disposition which the habit of doing good breeds and confirms. Even if no one else is better for our kindness, we shall be better because of the growing kindness in our hearts.

The Sage is leading us to understand a relationship with God in which we have the great capacity to hear and to respond to his will. He is subtly helping us to realize that we have a conscience, that as individuals we are responsible. I may say yes; I may say no. I am actually the driver of the chariot drawn by Plato's two horses, will and passion, and I am responsible to God. I am obligated to live under the law of love. The person achieving the Chief Good understands this truth and follows it. The happy person knows that when power is guided by the highest sense of justice that he or she is loving, and if love and justice are walking hand in hand in the life, he or she gets power through God who is the creator of the universe.

Such a person knows it is "God who works all" and that he is not responsible for events beyond his or her control. The happy person knows that it is his responsibility to do his duty of the moment whatever the wind may blow, and calmly leaves the issue in the hand of God.

The people who can trust God in this fashion know that the laws of nature will hold and be faithful in their course. The laws of nature will promote general good, even though, at the same time, they cause individual loss. When the clouds are full of rain they will empty themselves upon the earth. This brings fresh water to our reservoirs, yet it can also ruin a picnic and may endanger a harvest. When the wind is strong, it will blow down trees while it also scatters the seed which has been sown. The wise man, however, does not watch the wind and wait until it is too late to sow or watch the clouds and allow the ungathered crops to rot in the field. He is aware that although by human reason he knows a great deal, he ultimately knows little of the laws of nature and other works of God. He does not know how God puts his spirit in the child in the womb.

The happy man has learned the secret of wisdom. He knows that by giving, we gain. At a later period, Christ tells us the same truth. "If we lose our life, we gain it."

The happy man also learns that a man's true care is himself. He is responsible morally and, in this way, he not only has a conscience but he *is* a conscience. God breathed into the body and it became a living soul. All that pertains to the body, to the issues of labor, to the chance of future, is external to himself. Whatever forms these may take, he can learn from them and profit from them and be content in them. The happy man accepts that his true business in the world is to cultivate a strong and dutiful character which is faithful to conscience, which is guided by a high sense of justice which in the end even makes him loving. And this love must guide his use of power. This kind of character will prepare him for any world and for any fate. He will be able to live as a redeemed person in an unredeemed world, but he will also be prepared to live in a redeemed world. So long as a person can do that kind of living, his main duty will be done. When will, which involves power, and conscience, which points toward justice, are walking hand in hand in the heart of an individual under the power of God, the creator, the Kingdom of heaven, is near. You can cast your bread on the water looking for nothing in return. This is agape—this is love.

Again the Sage speaks to us and says that the happy man is like the farmer who sows his seeds in the morning and does not withhold his hand in the evening. He does not know which will prosper. The happy man sows his deeds of love in faith and leaves the results to God. The just, who use power according to their highest sense of God's own faithful justice, live by faith and walk by faith.

Finally, the Sage says rejoice, and every Jewish young person was encouraged to rejoice because the people held that their ultimate hope was in God.

Jewish young people were captured exiles, oppressed by despotic lords and rulers. These young people knew the Jewish law and tried to be loyal to it, but nevertheless, they were exposed to constant misfortune. All the blessings which the law pronounced on the obedient seemed to be withheld from them; all of its promises seemed to be false. The wicked triumphed over them and prospered in their wickedness. Where could they look for hope? We know from Psalms which were written in captivity that God's judgment of "no" was an incentive to hope and joy. Instead of fearing judgment, the pious Jews looked forward to it with joy and exultation. Psalm 96 (paraphrased) expresses this hope and joy:

> Let the heavens rejoice and let the earth be glad.
> Let the sea roar, and the fulness thereof.
> Let the field exult and all that therein is:
> And let all the trees of the wood sing for joy
> Before Jehovah: for He cometh,
> For He cometh to judge the earth,
> To judge the world with righteousness and the people with truth.

Love, faith and hope, these three, but the greatest of these is love. This love comes from God, who guides us by justice as known in the love of God expressed in Christ. When this happens, we are loving. When this love guides our use of individual and corporate power, we will be just in our individual as well as in our public life. In business, politics, and in our church institutions, we will seek the will of God. The person who achieves the Chief Good is a person who lives by love, faith, and hope. We cannot expect to find a more solid and enduring Good. These are the Eternal Good. The future shocks of change, the blows of circumstances, the mutations of time cannot touch the person who lives by love, faith, and hope. If trouble comes, that person can bear trouble and profit from it; if prosperity, success, and mirth come, he or she can bear these, too, and neither value them beyond their worth nor abuse them to the hurt of their personhood.

Chapter 9
The Problem
Is Solved Conclusively
ECCLESIASTES 12

Remember now your Creator in the days of your youth, for the Sage is the good student who has sifted all of the schemes and ways and aims of men. He has separated the wheat from the tares. He has taught us to know the wheat as wheat and the husks as husks. Husks may look like wheat, but husks do not have the food value of wheat and therefore cannot satisfy the keen hunger of the soul.

If you have followed the sifting process with the Sage to the close, you will find a great deal of husks scattered around your feet, but you will have a little wheat in your hand. From this little wheat a great harvest can grow. It will be a harvest unto life which is not to be found in wisdom, in pleasure, in devotion to business or public affairs, in a modest competence or boundless wealth.

We have learned that the person who achieves the supreme quest is the one who is loving, faithful, and hopeful—to say it another way, the happy person is one who is charitable, dutiful, and cheerful. He knows clearly that he is obligated to live under the law of love and consequently is loving and just through receiving power from God, his Creator. Remember, therefore, your Creator in the days of youth, for God is with you wherever you go. You are called to be conscious of present and constant judgment. Remember God and give to the poor and needy. Remember God and do all things as unto him. Remember God and your pleasures will grow sweeter for they are gifts of God. Take them in a thankful spirit for enjoyment. Living as unto God is the best safeguard against a life of selfishness.

Remember that the day of death will come. If you have lived without love, faith, and hope, the day of death will be a fearful experience. In order that we might understand this fear, the Sage describes the fear in the heart of people who experience a storm.

In such a storm, the sun and the light of the moon and the moon and the stars are darkened; the clouds return after the rain. In such a storm, the keepers or guards who guard the gates of the walled city tremble and strong men are bent with fear. The people who are grinding corn into meal and the wheat into flour are also afraid and stop their grinding. (This is like the Wheels of industry, stopping all at once in a big industrial city.) The silence is frightening. The storm has caused the grinding in this Eastern city to cease because the grinders are few, all of the frightened have run to cover.

The women live in the harem and see the outside world only by peeping through the windows. The storm is so great and the fear in their hearts so strong that they no longer are interested in peeping out of the window to see the outside world. They go and hide under the bed. Terrors are in the way and all the daughters of song are brought low. The almond tree can blossom and the grasshopper can live and drag himself along. (The almond and grasshopper were delicacies for food.) The storm is so fierce that the great and rich men lose their appetite—they are too frightened to eat.

This frightful experience in an oriental storm is the way

the Sage described the fear of death in the hearts of people who have failed to live above the sun. Death without God is a frightful experience. Remember, therefore, that this time of judgment will come to every person, the mourners will go about the streets, the silver cord of physical life will snap— the golden bowl will be broken—the pitcher will be broken at the fountain, the wheel broken at the cistern and the dust will return to the earth as it was and the spirit return to God who gave it. All will be empty if you come to that experience without love and faith and hope.

Being wise, the Sage taught people knowledge and wisdom through arranging many proverbs, to point people toward the life above the sun so that by faith they would live beyond the veil. He suggests that they live unselfishly (by the altar of sacrifice) through the word of God (table of shewbread) in a prayer fellowship (altar of incense) filled with the Spirit of God (golden candlestick).

Listen to these proverbs, "for the sayings of the wise are like goads, and like nails firmly fixed . . . which are given by one shepherd"; they deal with the problem and possibilities of human race. Listen to these nuggets of wisdom.

A bird in the hand is worth two in the bush; mere dreaming of nice things is foolish; it's chasing the wind.

A good reputation is more valuable than the most expensive perfume.

It is better to be criticized by a wise man than to be praised by a fool. For a fool's compliment is quickly gone as paper in a fire, and it is silly to be impressed by it.

Finishing is better than starting! Patience is better than pride! Don't be quick-tempered—that is being a fool.

Because God does not punish sinners instantly, people feel it is safe to do wrong.

But though a man sins a hundred times and still lives, I know very well that those who fear God will be better off.

See the way God does things and fall in line; don't fight the facts of nature. Enjoy prosperity whenever you can and when hard times strike, realize that God gives one as well as the other—so that every one will realize that nothing is certain "under the sun" in this life.

No one can hold back the spirit from departing. No one has the power to prevent death, for there is no discharge from that obligation and that dark battle. Certainly a man's wickedness in selfish living is not going to help him then.

There is hope only for the living. "It is better to be a live dog than a dead lion."

Live happily with the woman you love through the fleeting days of your life, for the wife God gives you is your best reward down here for all your earthly toil.

If the boss is angry with you, don't quit. A quiet spirit will quiet his ugly temper.

A dull ax requires more strength—be wise and sharpen the cutting edge.

When the horse is stolen, it is too late to lock the barn.

Laziness lets the roof leak and soon the rafters begin to rot.

Never curse the king, not even in your thoughts; nor the rich man either for a little bird will tell them what you said.

Live knowing that the whole earth is the Temple of God. As you live in this Temple, keep your ears open and your mouth shut! Don't be a fool who doesn't even realize it is sinful to make rash promises to God, for he is in heaven and you are only here on earth, so let your words be few. Just as being too busy gives you nightmares so being a fool makes you a blabbermouth. So when you talk to God and vow to him that you will do something, don't delay in doing it, for God has no pleasure in fools. Keep your promise to God. It is far better not to say you will do something than to say you will and then not do it. In that case your big mouth is making you sin. Dreaming instead of doing is foolishness and there is ruin in a flood of empty words. People will write many books—there is no end to this task and "much study is a wariness of the flesh."

Listen to the end of the matter: All has been heard. Fear God and keep his commandments. God has created us and we are obligated to live under the law of love. Each person is responsible for making the decision for surrendering to this obligation and becoming a conscience created by God. This is the whole duty of man. Fear God who has made himself known in Christ who is the bread and wine.

Christ, you will remember, was baptized with water. Water is raw material created by God. Man cannot make water. We can only accept water from God. Thus baptism itself teaches us that we can only accept salvation from God. Fear God who makes this salvation known in Christ. But Christ is also the bread and the wine. Bread and wine are the results of production out of the raw material which God has given so that we can become partners with God in creation.

Production is the bread and the wine. Production is the body of Christ broken, poured out, and shared with many. Production must not be carried on "under the sun." God created us to be partners with him in this great task of creation through production.

The way man uses production creates events in history. Many of these events have resulted in tragedy like hunger which comes through cut-throat competition. Cut-throat competition in production is not the body of Christ; it is the body of the devil.

Remember God will bring every deed of production into judgment, with every secret thing, whether good or evil. He will judge whether production has been the bread and wine, the body of Christ broken for many. The tragedy of our living under the sun is that the bread and the wine have been broken and given out for the few. Fear God, repent and cast your bread of production upon the waters, for you will find it after many days. Listen to the Sage. Hear God's "yes" to love and faith and hope so that production will become the bread and the wine in creative cooperation with God in life through love.

This is the end of the matter. Fear God and keep his two great commandments.

The Blood of Christ is poured out for the many and Christ will drink it new with us in his Father's Kingdom, which is at hand. This is a promise.

We will do well to listen to the Sage tell us about God's "no" for in recent history we have seen our interest in production which is devilish result in tragedies like our national involvement in Vietnam and our relative indifference to world hunger. For these God will bring us to judgment, for in reality the Kingdom of God is near. It is at hand to redeem our living "under the sun" so that the word of God directs our production for justice and peace.

Once again, hear the conclusion of the whole matter.

The people of wisdom are still searching for the good society. We look forward to the year 2000, and yet even our futurists tell us that we are still haunted by economic visions of the past. Adam Smith argued that a good society would result if government would leave individuals free to pursue their own specific interests with competition as the regulator and consumption as the goal. The Sage said this process in his day resulted in cut-throat competition and that it was empty.

Adam Smith viewed people primarily as self-interested individuals. Another individual, Karl Marx, saw people primarily as social beings and emphasized cooperation, equality, and consumption. He thought this would end human exploitation by self-interested people. The Sage tried the idea of cooperation as well. It failed also and he concluded that it, too, was empty.

In contrast to the optimism of Smith and Marx, the Reverend Thomas Malthus painted another grim pricture. Malthus was a reactionary in response to the French Revolution. He was heavily influenced by the past. His belief in original sin led him to view people as profligate, selfish, and unable to restrain their own appetites. This view was that they would breed until there was no longer enough food to go around. He taught that society is unable to regulate itself, except through famine, pestilence, plagues, disease, and war. Malthus' vision of the future was a nightmare.

When the Sage had a vision of this nightmare, he concluded "eat, drink, and be merry for tomorrow we die." In our time people perhaps look at the food problem, the energy crisis, and waste disposal and come to the same conclusion.

The Sage had the same situations and problems in his day and tried to move toward a new vision by saying, "Remember your creator . . . Cast your bread on the waters . . . Sow your seeds in faith . . . Rejoice in hope."

Today the disciples of Smith, Marx, and Malthus can argue that their visions are alive and well and that they still foretell the shape of things to come. The disciples of the Sage can argue that his vision is alive, too, because God is alive and he determines things to come. Can we say "yes" to the vision of God for the future?

Smith and Marx built a vision which had consumption as the goal of production. The Sage has given us a vision which has sharing as the goal of production. Christ gives us a vision which calls us to understand production as the bread and the wine.

Production can be the bread and wine of life when people involved in the marketplace accept Jesus Christ as the only judge, reconciler, savior, and lord of human beings. People responsible for production often get themselves confused with Christ. They become little gods and impose their visions upon human beings. They do not understand that Christ saves them as they become disciples of Christ in production.

The Sage says "remember now your creator." To the New Testament he is revealed in Christ who is the bearer and sender of the Holy Spirit. The Sage shows deep insight, for it is the grace of God in Jesus Christ which comes to us through the Holy Spirit. It is both forgiving grace, which accepts in us the potential for production and, at the same time, renewing grace which transforms and sanctifies production and makes it a blessing to all the people of the earth. The Holy Spirit creates the community in which the good life can be experienced. The Holy Spirit is the promise and anticipation of the new humanity which is already breaking in and will surely come through production becoming the bread and the wine.

Production which is done in the Spirit will be future-oriented toward the new humanity as it gives its attention to unity, deeds, and the future in Christ. The Sage points production toward the new vision. The vision of Adam Smith, Karl Marx, and Thomas Malthus did not include the new humanity. Any vision which excludes the new humanity will ultimately fail. Ecclesiastes speaks to our age. People who understand wisdom will listen to the conclusions given by the Sage on the whole matter.